Standards Based
Grammar

Grade 3

By David S. Dye M.Ed.

MODEL
CITIZEN
PUBLICATIONS

Model Citizen Publications,
Long Beach, CA 90808

This book is dedicated to my mother, Delores,
who is the hardest working person I've ever known...

...and to my wife, Joy, who is the most
loving, supportive person I've ever known.

For workshop / staff development information call
(562) 627-5662 or go to CreateBetterWriters.com.

ISBN-13: 9781492360735   ISBN-10: 1492360732

Table of Contents

Assessment Checklists   **1**

Unit 1   **3**
1. Unit Mastery Checklist · · · · · · · · · · · 4
2. Nouns · · · · · · · · · · · 5
3. Possessive Nouns · · · · · · · · · 12
4. Plural Nouns · · · · · · · · · · 19
5. Noun Review · · · · · · · · · · · 32
6. Unit Test and Answer Key · · · · · · · · 34

Unit 2   **39**
1. Unit Mastery Checklist · · · · · · · · · · · 40
2. Capitalization · · · · · · · · · · 41
3. Capitalization Test Review · · · · · · · 49
4. Unit Test and Answer Key · · · · · · · · 50

Unit 3   **53**
1. Unit Mastery Checklist · · · · · · · · · · 54
2. Parts of Speech Study Guide · · · · · · 55
3. Pronouns · · · · · · · · · · · · 56
4. Verbs · · · · · · · · · · · · 62
5. Adjectives · · · · · · · · · · 70
6. Contractions · · · · · · · · · 77
7. Test Reviews · · · · · · · · · · 83
8. Unit Test and Answer Key · · · · · · · 85

Unit 4   **89**
1. Unit Mastery Checklist · · · · · · · · 90
2. Comma Rules: Dates · · · · · · · · 91
3. Comma Rules: City, State / Address · · · 93
4. Comma Rules: Review · · · · · · · 95
5. Comma Rules: Lists · · · · · · · · 96
6. Comma Rules: Adjectives · · · · · · 99
7. Comma Rules: Friendly Letter · · · · 102
8. Comma Rules: Review · · · · · · · 105
9. Unit Test · · · · · · · · · · 109
10. Comma Rules Mastery Checklist · · · · · 110

Unit 5   **111**

1. Unit Mastery Checklist   112
2. Four Types of Sentences   113
3. Subjects and Predicates   119
4. Subjects   121
5. Predicates   124
6. Finding Subjects and Predicates   127
7. Test Reviews   131
8. Unit Test and Answer Key   135

Unit 6   **139**

1. Unit Mastery Checklist   140
2. Phrases   141
3. Fragment and Run-On Sentences   146
4. Titles or Topic Sentences   151
5. Subject-Verb Agreement   154
6. Test Reviews   158
7. Unit Test and Answer Key   160

Unit 7   **165**

1. Unit Mastery Checklist   166
2. Homonyms   167
3. Homonym Review   176
4. Compound Words   178
5. A vs. An   181
6. Unit Test and Answer Key   184

Unit 8   **189**

1. Unit Mastery Checklist   190
2. Friendly Letters   191
3. Unit Test and Answer Key   196

Unit 9   **197**

1. Unit Mastery Checklist   198
2. Prefixes   199
3. Suffixes   204
4. Test Review   209
5. Unit Test and Answer Key   210

Answer Key   212

About This Book

For years I've been looking for a grammar program that teaches the dozens of basic grammar rules my upper elementary school students need to know. Their lack of basic grammar skills left me with the feeling that they had to be seeing the rules I was teaching for the very first time. The blank stares I received when mentioning words like "possessive nouns" and "subject-verb agreement" had to mean that the teachers from my students' previous grades had never taught them. However, I soon realized, when reviewing grammar concepts only months after teaching them, I would receive those same blank stares again.

So what's the problem? Obviously I did not teach the concepts correctly, right? Maybe. I can say that many of my students would receive an A on most of my grammar tests. They could identify grammar concepts in worksheets and in Daily Oral Language. Unfortunately, these skills were not being transferred into their written and spoken language.

As a result, I have modified my grammar program every year of my teaching career for fourteen years. I have looked for a comprehensive grammar program that would help all of my students apply and retain the grammar concepts they need in order to speak and write effectively. I've used grammar programs provided by literature companies. I've spent hundreds of dollars on workbooks that teach specific concepts. I've spent hours creating worksheets to help my students master the English language. Despite all of this, I remained frustrated with the lack of progress my students were making in grammar.

What I wanted was a program that would help identify every skill my students should know by the end of the year. Also, I wanted to identify the skills my students should have mastered by the time they arrived in my class. Finally, I wanted to know what skills my students would be required to know in future grades so that I could introduce them to these concepts. It has become painfully clear that grammar is so complex that many students need a systematic program that allows them to master certain skills while preparing them for mastery of other skills. For students to master basic grammar, teachers of many grade levels will need to work together and create a plan.

The purpose of this book is to give teachers the plan they need to achieve the goals listed above. Grammar standards from grades three through eight (from the National Language Arts Framework) have been collected in an attempt to identify the basic skills our students need to master. In addition, extensive research has been done in an effort to identify specific lessons that will help build students' communication skills. As a result, not only does this book meet the national language arts standards for grammar, it goes far beyond.

Another benefit of this book is that it is systematic. It begins with the most basic of concepts and builds as you move through the units. Lower grades, or classes with students who are behind, can spend more time on certain concepts, while the upper grades can move more rapidly to get to the more difficult concepts. Furthermore, teachers can feel confident that the students are mastering the skills at their grade level while preparing them for instruction in the future.

You now have a fantastic system that will help build your students' language skills. With just fifteen to twenty minutes a day, students of all levels will grasp English like they never have before. English language learners, students with learning difficulties, and children who live in homes where English is not modeled correctly will benefit tremendously as they are taught English one step at a time. This program gives them a clear focus for the attainment of basic grammar. This is the ambition and the goal of Standards Based Grammar.

Using This Book

Below is a list of the special features in this book. If this is your primary grammar program, here is the basic procedure for the program:

A. Review each worksheet prior to the lesson. Focus on getting the students to understand the vocabulary. Begin each lesson by reviewing the vocabulary from the previous lesson.

B. Make sure students complete every journal extension. This helps students practice each grammar skill within the context of actual writing situations.

C. Do test review worksheets to prepare for each test.

D. Give the unit assessments. Correcting these can be time consuming. Many teachers correct these as a class.

E. Decide what you consider "Mastery". Record "Mastery" or "Non-Master" on the Parent Checklist for each student.

F. Transfer information from Parent Checklists to the students' Student Checklist. Your students can now take home their test and Parent Checklist.

G. Optional: Check off each skill taught on the Teacher Checklist. This will help you keep track of topics covered.

Features:

Grammar Standards Teacher Checklist

1. The Teacher Checklist allows the teacher to check off each standard after it has been taught. This is especially helpful if you do not teach the chapters in order or if you are using this book as a supplement. By doing this you are assured to cover every standard required for your grade level.

2. After each assessment you can keep a list of students who have "Mastery" and "Non-Mastery" of each standard. This will give you an idea of which standards need greater attention throughout the year. Additionally, this will provide wonderful feedback for future teachers. By making copies of this worksheet at the end of the year for future teachers, they will be well aware of the standards that give their new students problems.

Student Worksheets

1. Many concepts are taught on the first worksheet of each standard. The worksheets that follow allow practice in order to achieve mastery. However, it is crucial that you prepare ahead of time to deliver appropriate instruction of each concept.

2. The lessons on the worksheets are meant to be a springboard for your discussions about the grammar concepts. Most lessons can be reviewed quickly and taught with little preparation.

Features (Continued)

3. It is important that students have a chance to practice at home. Many worksheets have enough practice activities for the students to complete half at school and half as homework.

4. More worksheets may be required to achieve your goal of mastery. However, at least this program allows you to systematically identify when to teach a concept and when more help is required.

5. If more practice worksheets are needed, many teachers use the worksheets from their district's language arts program. Organize these worksheets based on where they are found in Standards Based Grammar.

Extensions

1. Many worksheets have "extensions" at the bottom. These are journal activities that help reinforce the concepts within the context of writing. This is an excellent way to help solidify the grammatical skills in the minds of the students.

2. In most cases, there is an extension on every other worksheet. Use the extension during your students' journal time, give it as homework, or complete it during class as an additional grammar activity.

Tests and Assessments

1. Every skill in each unit is assessed. Use the tests to keep track of student progress.

2. You can use whatever scale you feel is appropriate to grade the tests. For the difficult units, it is recommended that the standard grading scale be relaxed. One suggestion is to make the highest score an A, while the other students' grades are lowered from there.

Parent Checklists

1. This is a way for you to keep the parents involved in the progress of their child. After each test, check off the skills that have been mastered and the skills that have not been mastered. Send it home with the students.

2. This gives the parents the opportunity to practice these skills at home with their child. It may be helpful to direct the parents to a local teacher supply store where workbooks are available. Also, you can prepare packets of materials to send home for further practice.

Features (Continued)

3. In many cases, "Non-Mastery" may be checked for many or all of the skills taught. It is important that the parents understand that the goal of this program is to achieve mastery. While students may have a general understanding of a concept, mastery means a complete understanding and the ability to use the skill in the context of speaking and writing. Therefore, many parents might panic when they see so many skills marked "Non-Mastery." It may be helpful to put the students' test grade on the checklist to help ease the parents' anxiety. The parents will know that their child may not have mastered many concepts, but a C on the test will help them understand that their child is making progress.

Third Grade
Standards

Reading	Unit

Vocabulary and Concept Development

1.4 Synonyms, Antonyms, and Homonyms   (Unit 7)

1.8 Prefixes and Suffixes   (Unit 9)

Writing

Writing Applications

2.3 Write Personal and Formal Letters   (Unit 8)

Written Language Conventions

Sentence Structure

1.1 Use Complete Sentences   (Unit 5, 6)

Grammar

1.2 Parts of Speech / Compound Words / Articles   (Units 1, 3)

1.3 Past, Present, and Future Verbs   (Unit 3)

1.4 Subject – Verb Agreement   (Unit 6)

Punctuation

1.5 Punctuate Dates, City - State,
     Underline Titles of Books   (Unit 2 , 4)

1.6 Commas in Dates, Locations
     Addresses, Items in a List   (Unit 4)

Capitalization and Spelling

1.7 Capitalize Proper Nouns   (Unit 2)

1.8 Contractions / Common Homonyms   (Unit 3, 7)

3rd Grade
Grammar Standards
Teacher Checklist

		Mastery	Non-Mastery
	1. Parts of Speech: Noun Definitions and ID – Unit 1		
	2. Parts of Speech: Possessive Nouns – Unit 1		
	3. Parts of Speech: Plural Noun Spelling Rules – Unit 1		
	4. Capitalization – Unit 2		
	5. Parts of Speech: Pronouns – Unit 3		
	6. Parts of Speech: Verbs – Unit 3 (Past, Present, and Future)		
	7. Parts of Speech: Adjectives – Unit 3		
	8. Parts of Speech: Contractions – Unit 3		
	9. Comma Rules: Dates – Unit 4		
	10. Comma Rules: City, State / Addresses – Unit 4		
	11. Comma Rules: Lists – Unit 4		
	12. Comma Rules: Adjectives – Unit 4		
	13. Comma Rules: Letters – Unit 4		
	14. Four (4) Types of Sentences – Unit 5		
	15. Subjects and Predicates – Unit 5		
	16. Finding Subjects and Predicates – Unit 5		
	17. Phrases – Unit 6		
	18. Fragment and Run-On Sentences – Unit 6		
	19. Title or Topic Sentence? – Unit 6		
	20. Subject-Verb Agreement – Unit 6		
	21. Homonyms – Unit 7		
	22. Compound Words – Unit 7		
	23. A vs. An – Unit 7		
	24. Friendly Letters – Unit 8		
	25. Using Prefixes and Suffixes to Determine Meaning – Unit 9 un, re, pre, bi , mis, dis er est ful		
	26. Using Suffixes – Unit 9 er est ful		

3rd Grade
Grammar Standards
Student Checklist

_____

Student Name

		Mastery	Non-Mastery
	1. Parts of Speech: Noun Definitions and ID – Unit 1		
	2. Parts of Speech: Possessive Nouns – Unit 1		
	3. Parts of Speech: Plural Noun Spelling Rules – Unit 1		
	4. Capitalization – Unit 2		
	5. Parts of Speech: Pronouns – Unit 3		
	6. Parts of Speech: Verbs – Unit 3 (Past, Present, and Future)		
	7. Parts of Speech: Adjectives – Unit 3		
	8. Parts of Speech: Contractions – Unit 3		
	9. Comma Rules: Dates – Unit 4		
	10. Comma Rules: City, State / Addresses – Unit 4		
	11. Comma Rules: Lists – Unit 4		
	12. Comma Rules: Adjectives – Unit 4		
	13. Comma Rules: Letters – Unit 4		
	14. Four (4) Types of Sentences – Unit 5		
	15. Subjects and Predicates – Unit 5		
	16. Finding Subjects and Predicates – Unit 5		
	17. Phrases – Unit 6		
	18. Fragment and Run-On Sentences – Unit 6		
	19. Title or Topic Sentence? – Unit 6		
	20. Subject-Verb Agreement – Unit 6		
	21. Homonyms – Unit 7		
	22. Compound Words – Unit 7		
	23. A vs. An – Unit 7		
	24. Friendly Letters – Unit 8		
	25. Using Prefixes and Suffixes to Determine Meaning – Unit 9 un, re, pre, bi , mis, dis er est ful		
	26. Using Suffixes – Unit 9 er est ful		

Unit 1

Parts of Speech: Nouns

Noun Definition and Identification

Possessive Nouns

Plural Noun Rules

Grammar Standards – Unit 1

_____
Student

Parts of Speech

	Mastery	Non-Mastery
1. Noun Definitions and Identification		
2. Possessive Nouns		
3. Plural Noun Spelling Rules		

Grammar Standards – Unit 1

_____
Student

Parts of Speech

	Mastery	Non-Mastery
1. Noun Definitions and Identification		
2. Possessive Nouns		
3. Plural Noun Spelling Rules		

Nouns
Definitions
#1

In the next few chapters there are going to be many new words to memorize. Use the tricks recommended on the following pages to help you remember them all.

Nouns
The name of a person, place, or thing.

The Trick:
1. The word "noun" sounds like "nun." When you think of a noun, think of a nun.
2. A noun is a person, place, or thing. Think of a nun (person) going to a church (place) wearing a ring (thing).

In the space below, draw a nun in front of a church wearing a ring. Write the word "person" next to the nun, "place" next to the church, and "thing" next to the ring.

Chant: **"The nun went to the church wearing a ring: person, place, or thing."**

Directions: Write "person", "place", or "thing" next to each noun.

1. nun - _____
2. church - _____
3. ring - _____
4. park - _____
5. bike - _____
6. coach - _____
7. computer - _____
8. store - _____
9. driver - _____
10. school - _____
11. friend - _____
12. watch - _____

Nouns
Definitions
#2

Write the definition of a noun. Remember the trick.

Common Nouns

Common nouns DO NOT name
exact people, places or things.

girl, teacher, house, dog

The Trick:
Draw several nuns in a park. We do not
know any of their names.

Common Nuns

Proper Nouns

Proper nouns name EXACT
people, places, or things.

Amy, Mrs. Jones, White House, Fido

The Trick:
Draw a nun. Call her "Sister Mary". This
is the exact name of the nun.

Sister Mary, the Proper Nun

Directions: Underline all of the nouns in the sentences below. Write "common" or "proper"
above each noun.

1. Sister Mary gave graduation rings to Alejandra and Juan.

2. Our dog barked at Mrs. Ly, our neighbor.

3. His family went to San Francisco and drove their car across the Golden Gate Bridge.

4. Simm's Park will have a Halloween party and give away a lot of candy.

5. Mrs. Jones gave everyone in our class some pencils, paper, and folders.

Nouns
Definitions
#3

Write the definitions of common and proper nouns. Remember the tricks.

Common Nouns: _____

Proper Nouns: _____

I. Write a common noun for each proper noun below.

1. Sarah - ____**girl**____   6. Mrs. Jones - _____

2. Arizona - _____   7. Jones Bikes Shop - _____

3. Bugs Bunny - _____   8. Bible - _____

4. Olympics - _____   9. General Franks - _____

5. Grand Canyon - _____   10. Los Angeles - _____

II. Write a proper noun for each common noun below.

1. boy - _____   6. country - _____

2. dog - _____   7. song - _____

3. principal - _____   8. car - _____

4. actor - _____   9. name - _____

5. athlete - _____   10. store - _____

III. Write "Common" or "Proper" next to each noun.

1. BANANA - _____   6. DESERT - _____

2. TEXAS - _____   7. ENGLAND - _____

3. TIGER - _____   8. FARM - _____

4. DR. GEORGE - _____   9. MONOPOLY(game) - _____

5. DANIEL - _____   10. DRIVER - _____

Extension: Make a list of five (5) proper nouns. Write a matching common noun next to the proper noun just like in Part I above.

Nouns
Definitions
#4

Write the definitions of common and proper nouns. Remember the tricks.

Common Nouns: _____

Proper Nouns: _____

I. Write a common noun for each proper noun below.

1. Alexander - _____   6. Dr. Lee - _____

2. Mojave Desert - _____   7. Susie's Deli - _____

3. Porky Pig - _____   8. Frisbee - _____

4. Rose Parade - _____   9. Colonel Sanders - _____

5. White House - _____   10. Jupiter - _____

II. Write a proper noun for each common noun below.

1. girl - _____   6. city - _____

2. cat - _____   7. movie - _____

3. teacher - _____   8. bike - _____

4. singer - _____   9. video game - _____

5. artist - _____   10. restaurant - _____

III. Write "Common" or "Proper" next to each noun.

1. FLOWER - _____   6. MT. WILSON - _____

2. DOCTOR - _____   7. STORE - _____

3. LINCOLN TUNNEL - _____   8. COACH SMITH - _____

4. BEDROOM - _____   9. MARS - _____

5. BAMBI - _____   10. TRAINER - _____

Extension: Find a picture in a magazine. Make a list of all the proper nouns in the picture. Next, list ten (10) common nouns that you see.

Nouns
Definitions
#5

Singular and Plural Nouns

Singular Nouns name just one person, place, or thing.

<u>Examples:</u> girl, boy, dog, cat

<u>The Trick:</u> Draw a picture of one nun standing on first base. She just hit a single.

Plural Nouns name more than one person, place, or thing.

<u>Examples:</u> girls, boys, dogs, cats

<u>The Trick:</u> Plural sounds like squirrel. Draw a picture of a baseball field with a squirrel on each base. Remember that there are many squirrels on bases. They are the "plural squirrels".

Directions: Write "singular" or "plural" next to each noun.

1. nun - _____

2. squirrels - _____

3. rings - _____

4. toy - _____

5. people - _____

6. person - _____

7. car - _____

8. beds - _____

9. child - _____

10. children - _____

11. waiters - _____

12. ticket - _____

Nouns
Definitions
#6

I. Write the definitions for the nouns below. Remember the tricks.

Singular Nouns: _____

Plural Nouns: _____

II. Write "singular" or "plural" next to each noun.

1. trumpet - _____   11. flowers - _____

2. tacos - _____   12. geese - _____

3. baseball - _____   13. bottle - _____

4. bird - _____   14. mask - _____

5. flies - _____   15. players - _____

6. oxen - _____   16. cars - _____

7. house - _____   17. dream - _____

8. ships - _____   18. mice - _____

9. pilot - _____   19. dresses - _____

10. train - _____   20. shoe - _____

III. Look around the room. Make a list of five (5) singular nouns and five (5) plural nouns.

Singular	Plural
1. _____	1. _____
2. _____	2. _____
3. _____	3. _____
4. _____	4. _____
5. _____	5. _____

Nouns
Definitions
#7

I. Write the definitions for the nouns below. Remember the tricks.

Common Nouns: _____

Proper Nouns: _____

Singular Nouns: _____

Plural Nouns: _____

II. Write Person, Place, or Thing next to each word.

1. football - _____   5. field - _____

2. living room - _____   6. waiter - _____

3. quarterback - _____   7. love - _____

4. game - _____   8. park - _____

III. Write common or proper next to each noun. Next, tell whether the noun is singular or plural.

	Common / Proper	Singular / Plural
1. Mr. Jones	**Proper**	singular
2. teachers	_____	_____
3. pencils	_____	_____
4. Great Lakes	_____	_____
5. horse	_____	_____
6. balloons	_____	_____
7. Ryan	_____	_____
8. shoes	_____	_____
9. Statue of Liberty	_____	_____
10. cheerleader	_____	_____

Name: _____

Possessive Nouns

When a noun owns, or possesses, another item it is called a possessive noun.

Examples: John owns a book = John's book   The toys own a box = toys' box

Notice the apostrophe ('s) on John's book and the (s') on toys' box.

The apostrophe (') helps the noun show ownership.

Singular Nouns: Add ('s) to make the possessive. Rewrite the entire phrase below.

1. John_'s_ book

___**John's book**___

2. plane____ wing

_____

3. bike____ wheel

_____

4. door____ handle

_____

5. Tom____ friend

_____

6. room___ light

_____

Directions: Write each possessive from above in a sentence. Draw an arrow from the possessive to the noun it possesses.

1. (John's book) - _____

2. (plane's wing) - _____

3. (bike's wheel) - _____

4. (door's handle) - _____

5. (Tom's friend) - _____

6. (room's light) - _____

Nouns
Possessive Nouns
#2

Plural Possessive Nouns

For singular nouns, the apostrophe (') and "s" have been added to the word.

Examples: toy's box   dog's bone   car's tires   girl's idea

For plural possessive nouns, the "s" is part of the word. Therefore, just add the apostrophe (').

Examples: several cats' owner   many crayons' box   players' coach

Plural Nouns: Just add (') to make the possessive. Rewrite the entire phrase below.

1. bees_'__ hive   2. friends____ parents   3. bikes____ wheels

___**bees' hive**___   _____   _____

4. planes____ wings   5. books____ covers   6. rooms___ lights

_____   _____   _____

Plural Nouns that do NOT end in "s": Add ('s) to make the possessive. Rewrite the entire phrase below.

1. men_'s__ room   2. children____ toy   3. women____ club

___**men's room**___   _____   _____

4. deer____ meadow   5. geese____ pond   6. people___ houses

_____   _____   _____

Directions: Write each possessive below in a sentence. Draw an arrow from the possessive to the noun it possesses.

1. (bees' hive) - _____
2. (children's toy) - _____
3. (bikes' wheels) - _____
4. (deer's meadow) - _____
5. (books' covers) - _____
6. (people's house) - _____

Name: _____

Possessive Noun Trick

"Possessive" is a tricky word. It simply means "to own". You have already learned that "noun" sounds like "nun". Therefore, draw a picture of a nun holding a book. Draw her holding the book tightly because it is HER book and she's very "possessive" of it.

Memorize:

The nun is very POSSESSIVE of her book.

Directions: Write the singular and plural possessives for each phrase below.

	Singular	Plural
1. bell of the cow	cow's bell	cows' bell
2. toy of the child	_____	_____
3. bone of the dog	_____	_____
4. sports of man	_____	_____
5. thought of the king	_____	_____
6. purse of the woman	_____	_____
7. nest of the bird	_____	_____
8. idea of the family	_____	_____

Extension: Write any two (2) singular and any two (2) plural possessives from above in sentences.

Nouns
Possessive Nouns
#4

Write the definition of a possessive noun:

_____

I. Change each phrase below into a possessive.

1. The yard of Tim - __**Tim's yard**__

2. Houses of the cities - _____

3. Cupboard of the dishes - _____

4. Animals of the farm - _____

5. Movie of the actors - _____

6. The play of the children - _____

7. The friend of Amy - _____

8. The price of the dresses - _____

II. Tell what each noun below owns. Be sure to add the ('s) or (').

1. book - __**book's cover**_____   6. chair - _____

2. horse - _____   7. parks - _____

3. dogs - _____   8. songs - _____

4. driver - _____   9. flower - _____

5. trees - _____   10. car - _____

III. Write any two (2) possessives from above in a sentence.

1. _____

_____

2. _____

_____

Nouns
Possessive Nouns
#5

Write the definition of a possessive noun:

_____

I. Change each phrase below into a possessive.

1. The purse of the lady - _____

2. The wool of the sheep - _____

3. Computers of the lab - _____

4. Ideas of several girls - _____

5. Crust of the bread - _____

6. The game of the students - _____

7. The puppy of the brothers - _____

8. The rider of the horse - _____

II. Tell what each noun below owns. Be sure to add the ('s) or (').

1. pencil - _____   6. team - _____

2. frogs - _____   7. fish - _____

3. countries - _____   8. men - _____

4. song - _____   9. bikes - _____

5. folders - _____   10. house - _____

III. Write any two (2) possessives from above in a sentence.

1._____

_____

2._____

_____

Nouns
Possessive Nouns
#6

I. Make a list of twelve (12) items that someone or something might own on a farm. Be creative.

Examples: pigs' trough   farmer's tractor

1. _____

2. _____

3. _____

4. _____

5. _____

6. _____

7. _____

8. _____

9. _____

10. _____

11. _____

12. _____

II. Write a story about an exciting day on a farm. Use at least six (6) possessives from your list above.

_____

_____

_____

_____

_____

_____

_____

_____

_____

_____

_____

Name: _____

Nouns
Possessive Nouns
#7

I. Select a picture with a lot of action from a magazine or a poster. Write eight (8) possessives using the picture for ideas.

1. _____   5. _____

2. _____   6. _____

3. _____   7. _____

4. _____   8. _____

II. Write a story about the picture. Use the words from your list above.

_____

_____

_____

_____

_____

_____

_____

_____

_____

_____

_____

_____

_____

_____

_____

_____

Name: _____

Noun Spelling

 Rule # 1   If a word ends in "y", preceded by a consonant, change the "y" to "i" and add "es".

country - countries   mystery - mysteries   spy - spies   cry - cries
hobby - hobbies   beauty - beauties   lady - ladies   try - tries
melody - melodies   injury - injuries   sky - skies   copy - copies
berry - berries   supply - supplies   fly - flies

Rule # 2   If a word ends in "y", preceded by a vowel, just add "s" to make the word plural.

chimney - chimneys   turkey - turkeys   valley - valleys   birthday - birthdays
cowboy - cowboys

 Rule # 3   If a word ends in "f" or "fe", the "f" or "fe" is usually changed to "v" and "es" is added to make the word plural. <u>Chief</u> and <u>belief</u> are two exceptions.

half - halves   thief - thieves   loaf - loaves   life - lives
wolf - wolves   leaf - leaves   self - selves   knife - knives
calf - calves   wife - wives   elf - elves   shelf - shelves

 Rule # 4   If a word ends in "o", just "s" is added to make the word plural.

piano - pianos   photo - photos   solo - solos   rodeo - rodeos
banjo - banjos   patio - patios   igloo - igloos

* Sometimes exceptions are made plural by adding "es"
potato - potatoes   tomato - tomatoes   buffalo - buffaloes   tornado - tornadoes
hero - heroes

 Rule # 5   Some words form their plurals in unusual ways.

ox - oxen   foot - feet   tooth - teeth   mouse - mice
child - children   woman - women   goose - geese   deer - deer
sheep - sheep   man - men

 Rule # 6   If a word ends in "ss", "x", "z", "sh", or "ch" the suffix "es" is usually added to make the word plural.

tax - taxes   branch - branches   glass - glasses   fox - foxes
church - churches   guess - guesses   waltz - waltzes   buzz - buzzes
punch - punches   flash - flashes   hunch - hunches   crutch - crutches
patch - patches   lunch - lunches   bunch - bunches   touch – touches

Rules #1 and #2

Rule # ![1]   If a word ends in "y", preceded by a consonant, change the "y" to "i" and add "es".

Examples: fl<u>y</u> = fl<u>ies</u>   cop<u>y</u> = cop<u>ies</u>

Directions: Rewrite the singular nouns as plurals.

1. try - _____

2. hobby - _____

3. spy - _____

4. country - _____

5. mystery - _____

6. beauty - _____

7. cry - _____

8. lady - _____

Rule # ![2]   If a word ends in "y", preceded by a vowel, just add "s" to make the word plural.

Examples: turk<u>ey</u> = turk<u>eys</u>   vall<u>ey</u> = vall<u>eys</u>

1. chimney - _____

2. birthday - _____

3. cowboy - _____

4. donkey- _____

5. key - _____

6. toy - _____

7. monkey- _____

8. bay- _____

Directions: Write four (4) sentences using any four (4) plural words from this page.

Example: It took three <u>tries</u> for Santa to climb down the <u>chimneys.</u>

1. _____

2. _____

3. _____

4. _____

Rules #1 and #2
Part 2

I. Write Rules #1 and #2 below and give two (2) examples of each:

Rule #1 - _____

    Example #1 _____ Example #2 _____

Rule #2 - _____

    Example #1 _____ Example #2 _____

II. Rewrite the singular nouns as plurals. Write the number of the rule next to each word.

Rule #

___1___ 1. melody - ___**melodies**___

_____ 2. cowboy - _____

_____ 3. sky - _____

_____ 4. copy - _____

_____ 5. chimney - _____

_____ 6. donkey - _____

_____ 7. fly - _____

_____ 8. toy - _____

_____ 9. country - _____

_____ 10. hobby - _____

Rule #

_____ 11. birthday- _____

_____ 12. injury - _____

_____ 13. monkey- _____

_____ 14. berry - _____

_____ 15. supply - _____

_____ 16. bay - _____

_____ 17. mystery - _____

_____ 18. spy - _____

_____ 19. key - _____

_____ 20. lady - _____

Directions: Write four (4) sentences using two (2) plural words in the same sentence. Use one plural word from Rule #1 and one plural word from Rule #2.

    Example: It took three <u>tries</u> for Santa to climb down the <u>chimneys.</u>

1. _____

2. _____

3. _____

4. _____

Rules #1 and #2
Part 3

I. Write the **plural** forms of the words below in a sentence.

   1. (hobby / birthday) _____

     _____

   2. (fly / berry) _____

     _____

   3. (mystery / turkey) _____

     _____

   4. (lady / chimney) _____

     _____

   5. (supply / valley) _____

     _____

II. Write the **plural** forms of the words below three times.

   1. country - _____

   2. injury - _____

   3. cowboy - _____

   4. spy - _____

   5. bay - _____

   6. copy - _____

   7. beauty - _____

   8. melody - _____

Rules #1 and #2
Quiz

1. hobby - _____

2. turkey - _____

3. berry - _____

4. fly - _____

5. birthday - _____

6. cowboy - _____

7. injury - _____

8. copy - _____

9. chimney - _____

10. valley - _____

11. cry - _____

12. country - _____

13. mystery - _____

14. melody - _____

15. supply - _____

16. donkey - _____

17. spy - _____

18. lady - _____

19. toy - _____

20. beauty - _____

21. sky - _____

22. try - _____

Rules #3 and #4

Rule # 3   If a word ends in "f" or "fe", the "f" or "fe" is usually changed to "v", and "es" is added to make the word plural. <u>Chief</u> and <u>belief</u> are two exceptions.

Examples: hal<u>f</u> = hal<u>ves</u>   kni<u>fe</u> = kni<u>ves</u>

Directions: Rewrite the singular nouns as plurals.

1. wolf - _____

2. wife - _____

3. *belief - _____

4. thief - _____

5. self - _____

6. calf - _____

7. *chief - _____

8. life - _____

9. elf - _____

10. shelf - _____

Rule # 4   If a word ends in "o", just "s" is added to make the word plural. * Sometimes exceptions are made plural by adding "es": potato / tomato / buffalo / tornado / hero

1. banjo - _____

2. potato - _____

3. igloo - _____

4. rodeo - _____

5. tornado - _____

6. buffalo - _____

7. tomato - _____

8. solo - _____

9. hero - _____

10. patio - _____

Directions: Write four (4) sentences using two (2) plural words in the same sentence. Use one plural word from Rule #3 and one plural word from Rule #4.

Example: Three <u>wolves</u> chased the <u>buffaloes</u>.

1. _____

2. _____

3. _____

4. _____

Rules #3 and #4
Part 2

I. Write Rules #3 and #4 below and give two (2) examples:

Rule #3 - _____

    Example #1 _____   Example #2 _____

Rule #4 - _____

    Example #1 _____   Example #2 _____

II. Rewrite the singular nouns as plurals. Write the number of the rule next to each word.

Rule #   **Rule #**

__3__   1. leaf - __**leaves**__   _____ 11. rodeo - _____

_____   2. hero - _____   _____ 12. thief - _____

_____   3. wolf - _____   _____ 13. solo - _____

_____   4. patio - _____   _____ 14. tornado - _____

_____   5. buffalo - _____   _____ 15. loaf - _____

_____   6. knife - _____   _____ 16. life - _____

_____   7. self - _____   _____ 17. photo - _____

_____   8. banjo - _____   _____ 18. potato - _____

_____   9. tomato - _____   _____ 19. shelf - _____

_____ 10. half - _____   _____ 20. piano - _____

Directions: Write four (4) sentences using one plural word from Rules #3 and #4.

    Example: The <u>wives</u> took many <u>photos</u> of the children.

1. _____

2. _____

3. _____

4. _____

Rules #3 and #4
Part 3

I. Write the **plural** forms of the words below in a sentence.

1. (thief / piano) _____

_____

2. (elf / igloo) _____

_____

3. (knife / potato) _____

_____

4. (shelf / photo) _____

_____

5. (hero / tornado) _____

_____

II. Write the **plural** forms of the words below three times.

1. half - _____

2. banjo - _____

3. wolf - _____

4. tomato - _____

5. patio - _____

6. wife - _____

7. solo - _____

8. rodeo - _____

Rules #3 and #4
Quiz

1. calf - _____

2. piano - _____

3. potato - _____

4. wife - _____

5. loaf - _____

6. rodeo - _____

7. wolf - _____

8. thief - _____

9. patio - _____

10. self - _____

11. hero - _____

12. life - _____

13. tornado - _____

14. half - _____

15. banjo - _____

16. leaf - _____

17. igloo - _____

18. buffalo - _____

19. elf - _____

20. tomato - _____

21. shelf - _____

22. photo - _____

23. knife - _____

24. solo - _____

Rules #5 and #6

Rule # 5 Some words form their plurals in unusual ways.

ox - oxen   foot - feet   tooth - teeth   mouse - mice
child - children   woman - women   goose - geese   deer - deer
sheep - sheep   man - men

Rule # 6 If a word ends in "ss", "x", "z", "sh", or "ch" the suffix "es" is
usually added to make the word plural.

tax - taxes   branch - branches   glass - glasses   fox - foxes
church - churches   guess - guesses   waltz - waltzes   buzz - buzzes
punch - punches   flash - flashes   hunch - hunches   crutch - crutches
patch - patches   lunch - lunches   bunch - bunches   touch – touches

Directions: Rewrite the singular nouns as plurals.

1. goose - _____   8. sheep - _____

2. church - _____   9. lunch - _____

3. branch - _____   10. child - _____

4. deer - _____   11. tooth - _____

5. guess - _____   12. glass - _____

6. ox - _____   13. crutch - _____

7. fox - _____   14. mouse - _____

Directions: Write four (4) sentences using two (2) plural words in the same
sentence. Use one plural word from Rule #5 and one plural word from Rule #6.

Example: The <u>women</u> danced <u>waltzes</u> with the men.

1. _____

2. _____

3. _____

4. _____

Rules #5 and #6
Part 2

I. Write Rules #5 and #6 below and give two (2) examples:

Rule #5 - _____

    Example #1 _____ Example #2 _____

Rule #6 - _____

    Example #1 _____ Example #2 _____

II. Rewrite the singular nouns as plurals. Write the number of the rule next to each word.

Rule #

    Rule #

__5__   1. sheep - __**sheep**__

_____   2. patch - _____

_____   3. man - _____

_____   4. flash - _____

_____   5. ox - _____

_____   6. punch - _____

_____   7. guess - _____

_____   8. child - _____

_____   9. lunch - _____

_____   10. fox - _____

_____   11. tooth - _____

_____   12. deer - _____

_____   13. church - _____

_____   14. woman - _____

_____   15. branch - _____

_____   16. goose - _____

_____   17. glass - _____

_____   18. foot - _____

_____   19. tax - _____

_____   20. mouse - _____

Directions: Write four (4) sentences using two (2) plural words in the same sentence. Use one plural word from Rule #5 and one plural word from Rule #6.

Example: The <u>women</u> made <u>lunches</u> for the children.

1. _____

2. _____

3. _____

4. _____

Rules #5 and #6
Part 3

I. Write the **plural** forms of the words below in a sentence.

1. (ox / patch) _____

   _____

2. (goose / bunch) _____

   _____

3. (flash / deer) _____

   _____

4. (buzz / mouse) _____

   _____

5. (man / guess) _____

   _____

II. Write the **plural** forms of the words below three times.

1. sheep - _____

2. punch - _____

3. foot - _____

4. tax - _____

5. tooth - _____

6. waltz - _____

7. child - _____

8. branch - _____

Rules #5 and #6
Quiz

1. tax - _____

2. woman - _____

3. crutch - _____

4. punch - _____

5. touch - _____

6. mouse - _____

7. foot - _____

8. buzz - _____

9. deer - _____

10. lunch - _____

11. glass - _____

12. patch - _____

13. tooth - _____

14. guess - _____

15. ox - _____

16. sheep - _____

17. waltz - _____

18. fox - _____

19. hunch - _____

20. man - _____

21. bunch - _____

22. goose - _____

23. flash - _____

24. church - _____

25. child - _____

26. branch - _____

Noun Review
#1

Name: _____

I. Write the definitions of the following nouns:

Common Noun: _____

Proper Noun: _____

Singular Noun: _____

Plural Noun: _____

Possessive Noun: _____

II. Put an "x" below each word that fits the noun on the left.

	Singular	Plural	Common	Proper	Possessive
1. doctor's	X		X		X
2. Jeff					
3. cows					
4. New York's					
5. flower					
6. rocks					
7. brothers'					
8. road					
9. Arizona's					
10. Ms. Daisy					
11. clowns					
12. baskets					
13. hammers'					
14. sun					
15. Anna's					

Noun Review
#2

I. Put an "x" below each word that fits the noun on the left.

	Singular	Plural	Common	Proper	Possessive
1. Mt. Hood	_____	_____	_____	_____	_____
2. Mike's	_____	_____	_____	_____	_____
3. spoons	_____	_____	_____	_____	_____
4. children's	_____	_____	_____	_____	_____
5. Great Lakes	_____	_____	_____	_____	_____
6. ducks'	_____	_____	_____	_____	_____
7. game	_____	_____	_____	_____	_____
8. Play Station	_____	_____	_____	_____	_____
9. teachers'	_____	_____	_____	_____	_____
10. cities	_____	_____	_____	_____	_____

II. **Possessive Nouns:** Change each phrase below into a possessive.

1. cabin of the neighbor - _____

2. flower of the desert - _____

3. author of the stories - _____

4. animals of the farm - _____

5. movie of the actors - _____

6. feelings of your friends - _____

III. **Plural Noun Spelling Rules:**
   Directions: Change these singular nouns into plural nouns.

1. city - _____   4. toy - _____   7. fly - _____

2. church - _____   5. life - _____   8. monkey - _____

3. solo - _____   6. guess - _____   9. self - _____

Unit 1
Nouns Test

I. Noun Definitions: Put an "x" below each word that fits the noun on the left.

	Singular	Plural	Common	Proper	Possessive
1. book's	___	___	___	___	___
2. Amy	___	___	___	___	___
3. armies	___	___	___	___	___
4. Utah's	___	___	___	___	___
5. toy	___	___	___	___	___
6. bottles	___	___	___	___	___
7. sisters'	___	___	___	___	___
8. Hawaiian Islands	___	___	___	___	___
9. camera	___	___	___	___	___
10. Smith's	___	___	___	___	___

II. Possessive Nouns: Change each phrase below into possessives.

1. bone of the dog - _____

2. laughter of the students - _____

3. bottle of the baby - _____

4. laces of the shoes - _____

5. ideas of the women - _____

6. owner of the toy - _____

III. **Plural Noun Spelling Rules:**

Directions: Change these singular nouns into plural nouns.

1. hobby - _____

2. half - _____

3. turkey - _____

4. wife - _____

5. fly - _____

6. birthday - _____

7. wolf - _____

8. injury - _____

9. hero - _____

10. patch - _____

11. tooth - _____

12. solo - _____

13. country - _____

14. sheep - _____

15. mystery - _____

16. berry - _____

17. knife - _____

18. banjo - _____

19. cowboy - _____

20. tornado - _____

21. church - _____

22. child - _____

23. branch - _____

24. valley - _____

Unit 1
Nouns Test
Answer Key

I. Noun Definitions: Put an "x" below each word that fits the noun on the left.

	Singular	Plural	Common	Proper	Possessive
1. book's	X		X		X
2. Amy	X			X	
3. armies		X	X		
4. Utah's	X			X	X
5. toy	X		X		
6. bottles		X	X		
7. sisters'		X	X		X
8. Hawaiian Islands		X		X	
9. camera	X		X		
10. Smith's	X			X	X

II. Possessive Nouns: Change each phrase below into possessives.

1. bone of the dog - __**dog's bone**__

2. laughter of the students - ___**students' laughter**__

3. bottle of the baby - __**baby's bottle**__

4. laces of the shoes - ____**shoes' laces**____

5. ideas of the women - __**women's ideas**___

6. owner of the toy - ____**toy's owner**____

III. Plural Noun Spelling Rules:

Directions: Change these singular nouns into plural nouns.

1. hobby - **hobbies**

2. half - **halves**

3. turkey - **turkeys**

4. wife - **wives**

5. fly - **flies**

6. birthday - **birthdays**

7. wolf - **wolves**

8. injury - **injuries**

9. hero - **heroes**

10. patch - **patches**

11. tooth - **teeth**

12. solo - **solos**

13. country - **countries**

14. sheep - **sheep**

15. mystery - **mysteries**

16. berry - **berries**

17. knife - **knives**

18. banjo - **banjos**

19. cowboy - **cowboys**

20. tornado - **tornadoes**

21. church - **churches**

22. child - **children**

23. branch - **branches**

24. valley - **valleys**

Unit 2

<u>Capitalization</u>

Proper Nouns

Geographical Names

Historical Periods

Holidays

Special Events

_____

Student

Capitalization

	Mastery	Non-Mastery
1. Proper and Common Nouns		
2. Geographical Names		
3. Historical Periods		
4. Holidays		
5. Special Events		

Grammar Standards – Unit 2

_____

Student

Capitalization

	Mastery	Non-Mastery
1. Proper and Common Nouns		
2. Geographical Names		
3. Historical Periods		
4. Holidays		
5. Special Events		

Capitalization
Common and Proper Nouns
#1

Common Nouns: A common noun names any person, place or thing. Common nouns are <u>not</u> capitalized.

Person: girl   *Place: park*   *Thing: apple*

Proper Nouns: A proper noun names an exact person, place, or thing. Proper nouns <u>are</u> capitalized.

Person: Sally   *Place: Bloomfield Park*   *Thing: Kleenex*

Warning: Some words can be confusing. For example, "apple" is the specific name of a fruit, but is it a proper noun? Because there are many apples in the world, "apple" is not a proper noun. If we gave the apple a name–Bob, for example–Bob would be the specific name of the apple. Thus, Bob would be capitalized.

The Trick: Because common nouns name any person, place, or thing, you can usually put a or the in front of a common noun. Therefore, if you want to know whether a noun is common or proper noun, try putting "a" or "the" in front of it. If you can, it is probably a common noun. If you can't, it is probably a proper noun.

I. **Directions:** Write "Proper" or "Common" on the line. Next, rewrite the word. Capitalize the first letter if it is a proper noun. Finally, write "Person", "Place", or "Thing" on the next line.

Common or Proper?		Rewrite Word	Person, Place, or Thing?
__Common__	1. DOG	__dog__	__thing__
_____	2. MT. WILSON	_____	_____
_____	3. STREET	_____	_____
_____	4. BEAVER	_____	_____
_____	5. TEXAS	_____	_____
_____	6. SNAKE RIVER	_____	_____
_____	7. ISLAND	_____	_____
_____	8. BANANA	_____	_____
_____	9. TEACHER	_____	_____
_____	10. MR. DEAN	_____	_____

Capitalization
Common and Proper Nouns
#2

Directions: Write "Proper" or "Common" on the left line. Next, rewrite the word. Capitalize the first letter if it is a proper noun. Finally, write "Person," "Place," or "Thing" on the next line.

Proper / Common Noun	Rewrite Word	Person, Place, or Thing
_____ 1. HOME	_____	_____
_____ 2. PACIFIC OCEAN	_____	_____
_____ 3. DR. DREW	_____	_____
_____ 4. PIZZA	_____	_____
_____ 5. BANK	_____	_____
_____ 6. CIRCUS	_____	_____
_____ 7. OLYMPICS	_____	_____
_____ 8. PRINCIPAL	_____	_____
_____ 9. MARS	_____	_____
_____ 10. PENCIL	_____	_____
_____ 11. MEXICO	_____	_____
_____ 12. CLOCK	_____	_____

Extension: Where did your friends go? Write five (5) sentences about people you know. Tell the exact place where they went.

Example: Yesterday, Donna went to Downey.

Capitalization
Common and Proper Nouns
#3

Geographical Names: One type of proper noun is a geographical name.
This is the <u>exact name</u> of any place.

Examples: *Lake Tahoe   Big Bear   Grand Canyon   Hawaii*

Historical Periods: One type of proper noun is a historical period.
This is the <u>exact name</u> of any period of time.

Examples: *Middle Ages   Stone Age   Mesozoic Era*

Directions: Write **C** if the noun is a common noun; write **P** if the noun is a proper noun. If the proper noun is a geographical name, circle "GN". If the proper noun is a historical period, circle "HP".

__C__	LAKE	GN	HP	_____	PLANET	GN HP
__P__	LAKE TAHOE			_____	PLUTO	
_____	CITY	GN	HP	_____	RENAISSANCE	GN HP
_____	BELLFLOWER			_____	DECADE	
_____	JURASSIC PERIOD	GN	HP	_____	YOSEMITE	GN HP
_____	YEAR			_____	PARK	
_____	SACRAMENTO	GN	HP	_____	MEXICO	GN HP
_____	CAPITAL			_____	COUNTRY	
_____	SPRING	GN	HP	_____	AGE OF EXPLORATION	
_____	IMPRESSIONIST PERIOD			_____	CENTURY	GN HP

Extension: Write (5) five geographical locations (places) that are common nouns and five (5) that are proper nouns. Write them on a separate sheet of paper.

Example: park – Central Park

Capitalization
Common and Proper Nouns
#4

Holidays: Other types of proper nouns are holidays.
These are exact names of special days.

Examples: *Labor Day   Arbor Day   Christmas   Easter*

Special Events: Other types of proper nouns are special events.

Examples: *Miss America Pageant   Thanksgiving Day Parade*

Directions: Rewrite the words below. Be sure to capitalize the important letters. Next, if it is a holiday, circle "holiday." If it is a special event, circle "special event."

1. independence day - _____   Holiday   Special Event

2. lindstrom's talent show - _____   Holiday   Special Event

3. arbor day - _____   Holiday   Special Event

4. rose parade - _____   Holiday   Special Event

5. valentine's day - _____   Holiday   Special Event

6. beth temple bake sale - _____   Holiday   Special Event

7. memorial day - _____   Holiday   Special Event

8. thanksgiving - _____   Holiday   Special Event

9. opening day- _____   Holiday   Special Event

10. labor day - _____   Holiday   Special Event

11. kentucky derby - _____   Holiday   Special Event

12. christmas - _____   Holiday   Special Event

13. olympics - _____   Holiday   Special Event

14. lakewood's firework spectacular - _____

Holiday   Special Event

Extension: Select any five (5) holidays or special events from above. Write them in a sentence on a separate sheet of paper.

Name: _____

Capitalization
Common and Proper Nouns
#5

I. Circle the P if the noun is proper. Circle C if the noun is common. Next, rewrite the word on the line. If it is a proper noun, be sure to capitalize the first letter.

P   C   1. CENTRAL VALLEY - _____

P   C   2. BIRTHDAY - _____

P   C   3. ST. PATRICK'S DAY - _____

P   C   4. SPACE - _____

P   C   5. HANUKKAH - _____

P   C   6. SODA - _____

P   C   7. SNAKE RIVER - _____

P   C   8. MOUNTAIN - _____

P   C   9. IRON AGE - _____

P   C   10. BLACK HISTORY MONTH - _____

P   C   11. SPACE SHUTTLE - _____

P   C   12. OPENING DAY - _____

P   C   13. PARTY - _____

P   C   14. HALLOWEEN - _____

II. Write any four (4) proper nouns from above in a sentence.

1. _____

2. _____

3. _____

4. _____

Capitalization
Common and Proper Nouns
#6

Name: _____

I. Circle the P if the noun is proper. Circle C if the noun is common. Next, rewrite the word on the line. If it is a proper noun, be sure to capitalize the first letter.

P   C   1. NEW YORK - _____

P   C   2. FIRST COMMUNION - _____

P   C   3. PARADE - _____

P   C   4. ICE AGE - _____

P   C   5. NEW YEAR'S EVE - _____

P   C   6. MIDNIGHT - _____

P   C   7. CALIFORNIA - _____

P   C   8. RIVER - _____

P   C   9. EASTER - _____

P   C   10. THANKSGIVING - _____

II. Write two examples of each rule on the lines below. Use the list of words from above.

Geographical Names

1. _____   2. _____

Holidays

1. _____   2. _____

Special Events

1. _____   2. _____

Extension: Write any four (4) proper nouns from Part II in a sentence.

Capitalization
Common and Proper Nouns
#7

Name: _____

I. Directions: Write Proper or Common on the line. Rewrite the word with the proper punctuation below the word.

_____**Proper**_____	1. GRAND CANYON	_____	9. ROGET'S DICTIONARY
	Grand Canyon		
_____	2. RIVER	_____	10. KICKBALL
_____	3. MOON	_____	11. GRAND CANYON
_____	4. STATE	_____	12. FLORIDA
_____	5. PIZZA HUT	_____	13. ORANGE JUICE
_____	6. JUPITER	_____	14. CAKE
_____	7. MOUNTAIN	_____	15. WORLD WAR II
_____	8. JIMMY	_____	16. EGG

II. Directions: In the story below, circle all the common nouns. Cross out all the proper nouns and rewrite them with the correct punctuation below.

~~mom~~ and ~~dad~~ gave me an incredible (surprise) for my birthday last week. I crawled out
Mom   **Dad**

of bed that morning and expected to find a mountain of presents on our dinning room table.

Instead, my mom said, "Get dressed. We're going somewhere." My heart pounded as I wondered

where we could be going. The renaissance fair? The bugs bunny film festival? The empire state

building? The movies?

As my dad's chevy suburban pulled onto the golden state freeway, I thought I was going to die

with excitement. Before I knew it we were pulling off the freeway, and I could see the white mountain

of the matterhorn, a cool ride, rising into the sky. It was disneyland!

When we arrived at the park, many of my friends were there with presents in their hands and big

smiles on their faces. There was randy, helen, michael, lisa, and my cousin, skeeter. Everyone was

dressed in wonderful medieval period costumes. What a great surprise. After going on rides all day like

space mountain, big thunder mountain, and the haunted mansion, it was time to go home. What a great

birthday!

CreateBetterWriters.com   47

Capitalization
Common and Proper Nouns
#8

Name: _____

Directions: In the story below, cross out all the proper nouns, and rewrite them with the correct punctuation in the space below.

In the old west there's a story about a boy named the licorice kid. He may have been only ten years old, but he was the roughest, toughest, meanest hombre to walk the small desert towns of new mexico. Nobody knows where he came from, but many people say he just appeared one day out of a dusty wind coming down from texas. Riding on his trusty steed, buttercup, the licorice kid roams the vast fields of albuquerque rescuing strangers in need.

He earned his nickname one dry, hot day when the town bully, pokemon pete, returned from ballet camp. Pokemon pete immediately rounded up all the kids in the neighborhood and started forcing them to do ballet moves between the rolling tumbleweeds at sunflower park. Suddenly, there was the crack of a whip. It was the licorice kid, and he didn't look happy.

Pokemon pete, his braces gleaming in the blazing sun, squinted at the kid daring him to make his move. The kid squinted back and ripped a bite off his long red licorice whip. As the two slowly and deliberately marched their way toward each other, the tension was just too much to bear. A baby started to cry, jose hid behind his lemonade stand, and little girls clutched their tickle-me-elmo dolls to their chest.

The two stood facing each other, their arms arched by the sides of their levis, for what seemed like an eternity. No one moved a muscle. Wind whistled through the park and an eagle screeched overhead. Suddenly, pokemon pete made his move.

"I'll trade you a charizar for a piece of that licorice," he said with a deep, raspy voice.

"Sure," whispered the kid.

From that day on, pokemon pete was a new man. No more bullying. He traded his pokemon cards to get what he wanted.

Whatever happened to the licorice kid? No one knows for sure. Some say he rode a wells fargo wagon to california, offering licorice to gold miners near sacramento. But here in albuquerque, he'll always be in our hearts.

Extension: How many common nouns can you find in this story? Circle as many as you can find.

Capitalization
Common and Proper Nouns
Test Review

Directions: Write Proper or Common on the left line. Next, rewrite the word. Capitalize the first letter if it is a proper noun. Finally, write "Person," "Place," or "Thing" on the next line.

Proper / Common Noun	**Rewrite Word**	**Person, Place, or Thing**
_____ 1. CALIFORNIA	_____	_____
GN		
_____ 2. PACIFIC OCEAN	_____	_____
_____ 3. DOCTOR	_____	_____
_____ 4. WORLD WAR II	_____	_____
_____ 5. CITY	_____	_____
_____ 6. SAN DIEGO	_____	_____
_____ 7. PENCIL	_____	_____
_____ 8. BLACK HISTORY MONTH	_____	_____
_____ 9. MISS AMERICA PAGEANT	_____	_____
_____ 10. ALLIGATOR	_____	_____
_____ 11. COMPUTER	_____	_____
_____ 12. NEW YEAR'S EVE	_____	_____
_____ 13. BRIDGE	_____	_____
_____ 14. CAMERA	_____	_____
_____ 15. KENTUCKY DERBY	_____	_____

Extra Credit: For each <u>proper noun</u>, explain whether it is a **Geographical Name(GN), Historical Period(HP), Holiday (H), or Special Event(SE).** Write GN, HP, Holiday, or SE next to each proper noun from above.

Name: _____

Capitalization
Common and Proper Nouns
Chapter 2 Test

Directions: Write Proper or Common on the left line. Next, rewrite the word. Capitalize the first letter if it is a proper noun. Finally, write "Person," "Place," or "Thing" on the next line.

Proper / Common Noun		Rewrite Word	Person, Place, or Thing
_____	1. DRIVER	_____	_____
_____	2. STONE AGE	_____	_____
_____	3. BOOK	_____	_____
_____	4. THANKSGIVING	_____	_____
_____	5. DOLLHOUSE	_____	_____
_____	6. KITCHEN	_____	_____
_____	7. ATLANTIC OCEAN	_____	_____
_____	8. OLYMPICS	_____	_____
_____	9. PRINCIPAL	_____	_____
_____	10. ICE AGE	_____	_____
_____	11. CAFETERIA	_____	_____
_____	12. CHRISTMAS	_____	_____
_____	13. VIRGINIA	_____	_____
_____	14. OCEAN	_____	_____
_____	15. ROSE PARADE	_____	_____

Capitalization
Common and Proper Nouns
Chapter 2 Test - Answer Key

Directions: Write Proper or Common on the left line. Next, rewrite the word. Capitalize the first letter if it is a proper noun. Finally, write "Person," "Place," or "Thing" on the next line.

Proper / Common Noun		Rewrite Word	Person, Place, or Thing
Common	1. DRIVER	driver	Person
Proper	2. STONE AGE	Stone Age	Thing
Common	3. BOOK	book	Thing
Proper	4. THANKSGIVING	Thanksgiving	Thing
Common	5. DOLLHOUSE	dollhouse	Thing
Common	6. KITCHEN	kitchen	Place
Proper	7. ATLANTIC OCEAN	Atlantic Ocean	Place
Proper	8. OLYMPICS	Olympics	Thing
Common	9. PRINCIPAL	principal	Person
Proper	10. ICE AGE	Ice Age	Thing
Common	11. CAFETERIA	cafeteria	Place
Proper	12. CHRISTMAS	Christmas	Thing
Proper	13. VIRGINIA	Virginia	Place
Common	14. OCEAN	ocean	Place
Proper	15. ROSE PARADE	Rose Parade	Thing

Unit 3

Pronouns

Verbs: Past, Present, and Future

Adjectives

Contractions

_____

Student

Parts of Speech

	Mastery	Non-Mastery
1. Pronouns		
2. Verbs: Past, Present, and Future		
3. Adjectives		
4. Contractions		

Grammar Standards – Unit 3

_____

Student

Parts of Speech

	Mastery	Non-Mastery
1. Pronouns		
2. Verbs: Past, Present, and Future		
3. Adjectives		
4. Contractions		

Parts of Speech - Ch. 3
Study Sheet

Name: _____

Directions: Use this sheet to practice the parts of speech in this chapter. Fill it out as you study each part of speech.

Pronouns Pronouns take the place of a _____.

Study Picture

Examples: John = __**he**__ or _____

people = _____ or __**them**__

Tina's = _____

Verbs The three kinds of verbs are:

1. _____

Examples: _____

2. _____

Examples: _____

3. _____

Examples: _____

Study Picture

Adjectives   Adjectives describe a _____ or a _____.

Study Picture

Adjectives answer the questions:

1. _____

Examples: _____

2. _____

Examples: _____

3. _____

Examples: _____

Pronouns
#1

Pronouns A pronoun takes the place of a noun.

Examples: John = <u>he</u> or <u>him</u>

people = <u>they</u> or <u>them</u>

Tina's = <u>her</u> or <u>hers</u>

The Trick:
You already know that "noun" sounds like "nun". When you think of a pronoun, think of a "professional nun". Draw a nun with a hat that says "Pro". Draw another nun walking away because she's being replaced by a "professional nun".

Study Picture

What's wrong with the story below?

John was invited to Tina's birthday party. John wanted to get Tina a good present. However, John wasn't sure what to get Tina. Tina really likes stuffed animals, but John wasn't sure which one Tina would like. So John thought and John thought. Suddenly, John got a great idea. John would get Tina a gift certificate so Tina could select a bear Tina would really like. John was now very excited about Tina's birthday party.

1. Circle every "John", "Tina", and "Tina's" in the story above.

2. How many times is the word "John" used? _____ Circle all of the John's.

3. How many times is the word "Tina" or Tina's" used? _____

Extension: Rewrite the story from above. Keep the topic sentence. Next, replace John, Tina, and Tina's with the pronouns:

he, him, his, she, her, hers

Pronouns
#2

Subject Pronouns						
I	you	he	she	we	they	it

Object Pronouns

me	you	him	her	us	them	it

Possessive Pronouns

my	mine	your(s)	his	her(s)	our(s)	their(s)	its

Directions: Write all of the pronouns that can replace the nouns below. If you see (Your name: _____), write your name on the line.

1. Mr. Saito - _____

2. Rachel and Molly - _____

3. Candice - _____

4. our class - _____

5. (Your name: _____) - _____

6. pencil - _____

7. Tammy and (Your name: _____) - _____

8. football players - _____

9. book - _____

10. coaches - _____

11. Mrs. Morrison - _____

12. you and your best friend - _____

Pronouns
#3

Name: _____

Write the definition of a pronoun:

_____

Directions: Rewrite the sentences by changing the underlined nouns to pronouns.

1. <u>Lupe</u> gave a <u>present</u> to <u>Gena</u>.

   ____**She** gave **it** to **her**._____

2. The <u>dog</u> chased the <u>cats</u>.

   _____

3. <u>Nurses</u> give <u>medicine</u> to <u>patients</u>.

   _____

4. <u>Mom</u> baked <u>cookies</u> for <u>Tina and me</u>.

   _____

5. <u>Ron and I</u> snuck some <u>candy</u> into the <u>theater</u>.

   _____

6. <u>Dave</u> sent <u>Wilma and Betty's</u> clothes to <u>Mrs. Smith</u>.

   _____

7. <u>Coach Smith</u> made <u>the team</u> run laps around the <u>field</u>.

   _____

8. <u>Hillary and Bill</u> traveled with <u>Chelsea</u> to <u>George's</u> ranch.

   _____

Extension: Write the pronouns below in a story about someone grocery shopping. Remember, do NOT use a pronoun until you have stated the noun first.

| she | her | it | them | our |

Pronouns
#4

Name: _____

Write the definition of a pronoun:

_____

Directions: Rewrite the sentences by changing the nouns to pronouns.

1. <u>Dad</u> built <u>the bike</u> for <u>my brother</u>, and <u>my brother</u> really liked <u>the bike</u>.

_____

2. <u>Ralph and I</u> read <u>the book</u> to <u>our class</u>.

_____

3. <u>Gina and Linda's</u> grades were better than <u>Cindy's</u> grades.

_____

4. The <u>mail carrier</u> sent a <u>letter</u> to <u>Bob</u> by mistake.

_____

5. Making <u>Mike and Dawn</u> sing <u>a song</u> is like making a <u>pig</u> fly.

_____

6. <u>Donna's</u> joke made <u>Vince and Tommy</u> laugh so they retold <u>the joke</u>.

_____

7. This is <u>Greg's</u> book so put <u>the book</u> where <u>Greg</u> can find <u>the book</u>.

_____

8. <u>My friends</u> let <u>Heather and Sally</u> join <u>the club</u>.

_____

9. <u>The television</u> showed <u>dolphins</u> bouncing <u>a ball</u> on the <u>dolphin's</u> noses.

_____

10. <u>The Dodgers</u> play <u>the Angels</u>, but <u>Tom and I</u> can't see <u>the game</u>.

_____

Pronouns
#5

Directions: Fill in the blanks with a pronoun that fits.

1. __They__ gave all __their__ homework to __him__.

2. _____ like to play with _____.

3. _____ chewed a hole in _____ sock so I had to replace _____.

4. _____ played with _____ for an hour until _____ had to go home.

5. _____ cat likes to be scratched behind _____ ears.

6. _____ used _____ strong muscles to lift _____ over the fence.

7. _____ wrote _____ a letter and mailed _____ that night.

8. _____ didn't know that the toy was _____ so we gave it away.

9. _____ game needs batteries so I bought _____ at the store.

10. Coach told _____ that if _____ play hard then _____ would win.

11. _____ whistle was loud, and it hurt _____ ears.

12. _____ invited _____ to _____ party.

Extension: Write the possessive pronouns below in a story about a birthday party for you. Remember, do NOT use a pronoun until you have stated the noun first.

my   her   its   their

Pronouns
#6

I. Directions: Circle all of the pronouns in the story below. Can you find all 31?

The children had a great time at camp. First, they got off the bus and found their cabin. It was very nice. Then, the counselor said, "I want you to put your clothes on hangers then put them in the closet." He then gave them a ticket to get lunch. Later, the teacher took her students on a nature walk. When they returned, the staff showed them how to make crafts. One student asked the head counselor, " Can we take them home with us?" He said that we could take them home and show them to our parents. When the trip was over, the campers packed their suitcases. Amy couldn't find her craft until she was finished packing. It was in her friend's suitcase who knew it wasn't hers. Amy was happy to find it and show it to her mom when she got home.

II. When a writer uses many pronouns, it may be hard to understand the noun that the pronoun is replacing. The noun being replaced is called the **antecedent**. In the story above, draw an arrow from each pronoun to its antecedent. Feel free to use different colored crayons or colored pencils. It's going to get messy ☺ .

Example:

The children had a great time at camp. First, they got off the bus and found their cabin.

Extension: Write a story about someone playing a game. Use the five (5) pronouns below. When finished, circle your pronouns and draw an arrow to the antecedent. If each pronoun does not have a written antecedent, you need to fix your story so that it does have an antecedent.

| He | their | my | her | our |

Verbs
#1

Here are three kinds of verbs:

      1. Action Words   -   run, jump, play, love, wish

      2. "To Be" Verbs   -   is, are, was, were, be

      3. Helping verbs   -   <u>is</u> running, <u>are</u> jumping, <u>was</u> playing

---

The Trick: The word "verb" starts with the letter V. Make a V with your fingers. Turn it upside down and make an " with the finger on your other hand. The A stands for Action! * As you do this, say to yourself, "A verb," (Make the V) "is an action word." (Make the A)

I. How many action verbs can you think of that start with the letters below. Write at least five (5) for each letter.

C	P	S	T
<u>cut</u>	____	____	____
____	____	____	____
____	____	____	____
____	____	____	____
____	____	____	____

II. Circle the verbs in each sentence below.

1. Amy gave me a cookie.

2. Run to the store for some milk.

3. I want an ice cream.

4. The students behind me waited for three hours.

5. She was happy so she brought me some flowers.

6. We are camping at the park.

Verbs
#2

A verb shows _____

     Examples: sing, run, jump

I. How many action verbs can you write that start with the letters below.
Write at least five (5) for each letter.

A	R	M	G
_____	_____	_____	_____
_____	_____	_____	_____
_____	_____	_____	_____
_____	_____	_____	_____
_____	_____	_____	_____

II. Fill in the blank with a verb that fits the sentence.

1. The teacher _____ the students a test.

2. She _____ all of the cookies.

3. He will _____ in the first race and _____ the second race.

4. I _____ for my sister after school so I can _____ home with her.

5. I _____ a letter to my friend, and my mom _____ it.

6. Grandpa said he would _____ me a dollar if I _____ a song.

7. Tanya _____ eating some watermelon under the tree.

8. They _____ excited about their chance to _____ to Disneyland.

9. Airplanes _____ over our house every day.

10. In baseball it is important to _____ the ball and _____ quickly.

Extension: Write any five (5) verbs from Part I in a sentence.

Verbs
#3

Name: _____

Verbs are action words. We can use them to talk about action that has taken place in the past, action that is taking place now, or action that will be taking place in the future. As a result, verbs have a past, present and future **tense**.

Past Tense	Present Tense	Future Tense
talked	talk	will talk
ran	run	will run

I. Write the past, present, and future tense for the words below.

	Past Tense	Present Tense	Future Tense
1. talk -	_____	_____	_____
2. walked -	_____	_____	_____
3. know -	_____	_____	_____
4. will look -	_____	_____	_____
5. spoke -	_____	_____	_____
6. arrive -	_____	_____	_____
7. sit -	_____	_____	_____
8. will teach -	_____	_____	_____

II. Write "past," "present," or "future" depending on the tense of the verb.

1. play - _____

   will play - _____

   played - _____

2. sang - _____

   sing - _____

   will sing - _____

3. climb - _____

   will climb - _____

   climbed - _____

4. ate - _____

   eat - _____

   will eat - _____

5. jump - _____

   will jump - _____

   jumped - _____

6. will swim - _____

   swam - _____

   swim - _____

CreateBetterWriters.com

64

Name: _____

Verbs
#4

I. Write the past, present, and future tense for the words below.

	Past Tense	Present Tense	Future Tense
1. sing -	_____	_____	_____
2. thought -	_____	_____	_____
3. love -	_____	_____	_____
4. will type -	_____	_____	_____
5. fight -	_____	_____	_____
6. left -	_____	_____	_____
7. hit -	_____	_____	_____
8. will sail -	_____	_____	_____

II. Write "past," "present," or "future" depending on the tense of the verb.

1. fly - _____

    will fly - _____

2. danced - _____

    dance - _____

3. wish - _____

    will wish - _____

4. go - _____

    went - _____

5. hurried - _____

    will hurry - _____

6. will borrow - _____

    borrowed - _____

Extension: A common mistake for young writers is to mix the tenses in a story. Sometimes they start writing the story as if something is currently happening. Then they switch in the middle of the story and start writing as if something has already happened.

Write a three (3) sentence story (one paragraph maximum) about something that happened to you earlier in the week. Next, rewrite the story as if it is happening to you right now. Finally, rewrite the story a third time. Pretend that you are predicting what will happen to you some time in the future.

Verbs
#5

When is a verb not an action word? When the verb is "being". Here are five (5) words that show action by saying that something is just "being".

is   are   was   were   am

Examples:

He **is** happy.   They **are** happy.

She **was** happy.   We **were** happy.

I **am** happy.

Directions: Fill in the blanks with the correct "being" verb.

is   are   was   were   am

1. I _____ a good student.

2. We _____ sad about the sick child.

3. _____ they hungry for more pizza?

4. He _____ our class president.

5. Tina and Amy _____ cheerleaders.

6. Last week he _____ angry about the accident.

7. _____ I in trouble?

8. Yesterday, he _____ late for school.

9. The puppy _____ lonely when we went to school.

10. _____ the teacher ready to teach?

Extension: Write five (5) sentences using the "to be" verbs:

is   are   was   were   am

Verbs
#6

I. List five (5) action verbs and five (5) "to be" verbs:

Action Verbs: _____ _____ _____ _____ _____

"To-Be" Verbs: _____ _____ _____ _____ _____

Helping Verbs: Helping verbs help the main verb give a more accurate meaning.

Verb Phrase: The helping verb(s) join the main verb to make a verb phrase.

Examples:

Helping Verb(s)	+	**Main Verb**	=	**Verb Phrase**
is		playing		is playing
should have		waited		should have waited
would have been		late		would have been late

Helping Verbs

is	are	was	were	am
be	been	being	can	could	did	do
does	had	has	have	may	might
must	shall	should	will	would

Directions: List three verb phrases for each action verb below. Use the helping verbs in the box above.

1. play - **can play** , **does play** , **will play**

2. working - _____ , _____ , _____

3. stopped - _____ , _____ , _____

4. smell - _____ , _____ , _____

5. written - _____ , _____ , _____

6. laughing - _____ , _____ , _____

Verbs
#7

I. Directions: List three verb phrases for each action verb below. Use the helping verbs from Verbs #6 for ideas.

1. sing - __could sing__ , __must sing__ , __would sing__

2. crying - _____ , _____ , _____

3. shopped - _____ , _____ , _____

4. sung - _____ , _____ , _____

5. fight - _____ , _____ , _____

6. helped - _____ , _____ , _____

7. typing - _____ , _____ , _____

8. baked - _____ , _____ , _____

II. "To Be" Verb or Helping Verb?

Remember, a helping verb must help another verb. If the verb is not helping another verb, it is the main verb.

Directions: In the sentences below, underline the verb or verb phrase. Write "Helping" if there is a helping verb in the sentence. Write "To Be" if it is the main verb.

__Helping__ 1. She is asking the teacher a question.

__To Be__ 2. Tom was happy to be home.

_____ 3. Mom is making a cake for our party.

_____ 4. I am tired of cartoons.

_____ 5. Dad was singing in the shower.

_____ 6. They were the leaders of our student council.

_____ 7. We are making pictures for the art contest.

_____ 8. He was the strongest person on our team.

Extension: Write three (3) sentences using the words below as **"to be"** verbs. Write three (3) sentences using the words below as **helping** verbs.

is are was

Verbs
#8

Name: _____

I. In the sentences below, underline the verb or verb phrase. Write "Helping" if there is a helping verb in the sentence. Write "To Be" if the to-be verb is the main verb. Write "Action" if it is an action verb.

__Action__ 1. Mom <u>made</u> a cake for my birthday.

_____ 2. Jill is sad about Jack's broken crown.

_____ 3. The children were complaining about the food.

_____ 4. We drove all the way to Florida.

_____ 5. I am making a dress for my sister.

_____ 6. The boys wrestled in the back yard for an hour.

_____ 7. Mr. Starr is the driver of the bus.

_____ 8. Mom is shopping with my aunt.

_____ 9. They were ready for the game.

_____ 10. Amy wrote a nice, friendly letter to her cousin.

_____ 11. She is looking for her sweater.

_____ 12. The baby will drink his milk after his nap.

II. Write a story about a party using the helping verbs, "to be" verbs, and action verbs listed below.

Helping verbs: should be waiting   will bring
"To Be" verbs: is   am
Action verbs: opened   wrapped

_____

_____

_____

_____

_____

_____

_____

_____

Adjectives
#1

> **Adjectives** are words that describe nouns.
>
> Examples: <u>Big</u> basket   <u>Several</u> buildings   <u>Three</u> clowns
>
> Adjectives answer three questions:
> 1. **What kind?** <u>What kind</u> of basket? <u>Big</u> Basket
> 2. **How Much?** How much money? <u>Several</u> dollars
> 3. **How Many?** How many clowns? <u>Three</u> clowns

I. Below is a list of adjectives. Write "What kind?", "How Much", or "How Many" next to each adjective.

1. big - _____
2. several - _____
3. four - _____
4. many - _____
5. hungry - _____

6. pretty - _____
7. small - _____
8. skinny - _____
9. tall - _____
10. some - _____

II. Write three adjectives to describe each noun below.

1. elephant - _____ _____ _____
2. pillow - _____ _____ _____
3. ocean - _____ _____ _____
4. dog - _____ _____ _____
5. your neighbor's hair - _____ _____ _____
6. your best friend - _____ _____ _____
7. your shirt - _____ _____ _____
8. your bedroom - _____ _____ _____
9. snake - _____ _____ _____
10. circus - _____ _____ _____

Adjectives
#2

I. Below is a list of adjectives. Write "What kind?" "How Much," or "How Many" next to each adjective.

1. large - _____   6. weird - _____

2. few - _____   7. wet - _____

3. seven - _____   8. hairy - _____

4. many - _____   9. short - _____

5. slimy - _____   10. a lot - _____

II. Write three adjectives to describe each noun below.

1. puppy - _____ _____ _____

2. pizza - _____ _____ _____

3. mountains - _____ _____ _____

4. your favorite story - _____ _____ _____

5. a family member - _____ _____ _____

6. your classroom - _____ _____ _____

7. your shoes - _____ _____ _____

8. a concert - _____ _____ _____

9. trash can - _____ _____ _____

10. cotton candy - _____ _____ _____

Extension: Select any five (5) nouns from Part II and write them in sentences. Be sure to use at least one of the adjectives to describe them.

Example: The soft, cuddly puppy played on the floor.

Adjectives
#3

I. Directions: Write an adjective on each line below that fits the sentence.

1. We spent an hour trying to clean the _____ carpet.

2. The girl's _____, _____ hair blew in the wind.

3. I got a _____ present for my birthday. It was a _____ bike.

4. My _____ little sister drove me crazy with her _____ noises.

5. I think that this _____ milk is rotten.

6. We cuddled under our _____, _____ blanket.

7. The _____ clowns sprayed water in the ring master's face.

8. Mom said, "Clean this _____ room right now!"

9. My sister wears the same _____ dress every Friday.

10. The tree was covered with _____, _____ lights.

11. A _____, _____ toad hopped across our yard.

12. At the beach we made _____ sand castles.

II. Write at least five (5) sentences about being in a garden. Describe what you see. Be sure to put at least one adjective in each sentence.

_____

_____

_____

_____

_____

_____

_____

_____

_____

_____

Adjectives
#4

I. Directions: Write an adjective on each line below that fits the sentence.

1. The circus had a _____ elephant and a bunch of _____ monkeys.

2. Our class was so _____ when the principal walked in.

3. For picture day we all wore _____, _____ clothes.

4. A _____ spider made a _____ web in our yard.

5. Andy is a _____ player, but he is too _____ .

6. I just love my _____, _____ pillow.

7. The _____ house felt good after being in the _____ rain.

8. We read a _____ story about a _____ pirate.

9. The climbers kept falling on the _____ ice.

10. The _____ seals made _____ noises so we'd throw them some fish.

11. There was a _____, _____ bear eating our food.

12. Dad warned, "Watch out for _____ animals on your hike."

II. Think of an adjective for each noun below. Write the adjective and noun in a sentence.

1. beach - _____

    _____

2. teddy bear - _____

    _____

3. watermelon - _____

    _____

4. whistle - _____

    _____

Adjectives
#5

Comparatives and Superlatives

Adjectives that compare **two things** are called **comparatives**.
Adjectives that compare **three or more things** are called **superlatives**.

Comparatives can be made in two ways:
1. Add "er" to the one syllable adjectives.   bigg<u>er</u>, strong<u>er</u>, fast<u>er</u>
2. Add "more" to some two syllable adjectives and all three or more syllable words.   more helpful, more famous

Superlatives can also be made in two similar ways:
1. Add "est" to the one syllable adjectives. bigg<u>est</u>, strong<u>est</u>, fast<u>est</u>
2. Add "more" to some two syllable adjectives and all three or more syllable words.   most helpful, most famous

I. Fill in the blank with the correct form of each word. *Words break the general rules.

Adjective	Comparative	Superlative
1. intelligent	more intelligent	most intelligent
2. big		
3. calm		
4. powerful		
5. *messy		
6. dark		
7. exciting		
8. *risky		
9. curious		
10. *angry		
11. small		
12. dangerous		

Adjectives
#6

I. Fill in the blanks with the correct form of each word.

Adjective	Comparative	Superlative
1. good	_____better_____	_____best_____
2. new	_____	_____
3. intelligent	_____	_____
4. patient	_____	_____
5. *grouchy	_____	_____
6. cheap	_____	_____
7. patriotic	_____	_____
8. *dumpy	_____	_____

* What do you notice about all the adjectives that end in Y ?

_____

II. Circle the correct word in each pair. On the line, tell if it is comparative or superlative.

Comparative or Superlative?

__Superlative__ 1. This is the (darker , (darkest)) cave of all.

_____ 2. I think turkey is (more tasty , tastier) than ham.

_____ 3. This is the (cleaner , cleanest) shirt in my closet.

_____ 4. Tommy is a (gooder , better) reader than I.

_____ 5. This is the (most funny , funniest) movie I've ever seen.

_____ 6. A snake is (more dangerous , most dangerous) than a spider.

_____ 7. Julie being absent is (more surprising , most surprising) than Kim being late.

_____ 8. Juan is the (nicer , nicest) person in the world.

Extension: Write three (3) sentences about your school using comparatives and three (3) sentences using superlatives. You may use any comparatives and superlatives on this page or make up your own.

Adjectives
#7

I. Directions: Write an adjective on each line below that fits the sentence.

1. The _____ man waited for me to count my money.

2. A _____, _____ balloon floated over our heads.

3. We caught a _____ fish on our camping trip.

4. While hiking we saw a _____ skunk in the bushes.

5. The show was so _____ we laughed for hours.

6. The ball hit the window and sent _____, _____ pieces of glass onto the floor.

7. The bread was too _____ for anyone to eat.

II. Fill in the blanks with the proper comparative or superlative.

(strong)   1. Superman is the _____ person in the world.

(old)   2. My brother is _____ than me.

(messy)   3. Her room is _____ than his room.

(exciting)   4. This is the _____ story I've ever read.

(cheap)   5. A used car is _____ than a new car.

(dangerous) 6. The crocodile is the _____ animal in the river.

(cool)   7. It will be _____ if you sit in the shade.

(intelligent) 8. Patricia is the _____ person at our school.

Extension: Write a story about a fun day at a carnival. Use the adjectives below in your story.

sweet   fast   sour   crunchy   loud

Contractions #1

> **Definition:** "Contract" means "to shorten." Therefore, a contraction is when two words are shortened into one word. An apostrophe is used to show where letters from one of the words were left out.

Examples: he + is = he's   John + is = John's   you + are = you're

⬆ missing i   ⬆ missing i   ⬆ missing a

I. The words below are often used to form contractions. Turn the contractions back into the two words.

not   are   will   have   is   am   had   would

1. he'd - _____**he would**_____   6. aren't - _____

2. they're - _____   7. don't - _____

3. I'm - _____   8. it'll - _____

4. you'll - _____   9. should've - _____

5. we're - _____   10. hasn't - _____

II. Turn the words below into contractions.

1. he will - _____**he'll**_____   6. could not - _____

2. they have - _____   7. I have - _____

3. have not - _____   8. she is - _____

4. we will - _____   9. *will not - _____

5. it is - _____   10. cannot - _____

Contractions #2

Directions: Use the words in the box below to make as many contractions as possible for each word listed.

```
┌─────────────────────────────┐
│   not    would    am        │
│   are    had           is   │
│        will    have         │
└─────────────────────────────┘
```

Example:

She - __she'd__ (she would) __she'd__ (she had) __she'll__ __she's__

1. he - _____ _____ _____ _____

2. they - _____ _____ _____ _____ _____

3. I - _____ _____ _____ _____

4. you - _____ _____ _____ _____ _____

5. we - _____ _____ _____ _____ _____

6. could - _____ _____   11. will - _____

7. it - _____ _____   12. are - _____

8. should - _____ _____   13. has - _____

9. would - _____ _____   14. did - _____

10. do - _____   15. have - _____

Extension: Write five (5) sentences using the contractions below.

it's   don't   you're   we'll   I'm

Contractions
#3

Two Tricky Contractions

What words make up **can't** and **won't**?

Can't should be "can not" and won't should be "wo not". Here's how they really look: **can't = cannot**   **won't = will not**

I. Write "cannot" or "will not" on the lines below. Next, write "can't" or "won't" below the line.

1. She ___**cannot**___ help me with my homework.
   can't

2. The cake _____ be ready until 8:00.

3. Our kitten _____ get out of the tree.

4. The boss _____ take "no" for an answer.

5. I _____ study with the television on.

6. The children _____ play with you if you are not nice.

7. Johnny is sick so he _____ go to school.

8. No matter how hard I scrub, the stain _____ come out.

9. The baby _____ sleep because he's sick.

10. Cindy _____ come out of the bathroom.

II. Change the contractions below into two words.

1. Amy's - _____**Amy is**_____   6. won't - _____

2. John'll - _____   7. hasn't - _____

3. can't - _____   8. I'm - _____

4. they're - _____   9. would've - _____

5. you've - _____   10. we're - _____

Name: _____

Contractions
#4

Contraction Danger

Be careful never to use negative words like **no, never**, and **nothing** with a contraction that ends in **n't**.

Incorrect	**Correct**
She would**n't** like **no** ice cream.	She would**n't** like **any** ice cream.
He **doesn't never** lie.	He **doesn't ever** lie.
They **aren't** doing **nothing** tonight.	They **aren't** doing **anything** tonight.

I. Rewrite each sentence correctly.

1. We don't need to bring nothing to the party.

   _____

2. Hazel won't let nobody ride her bike.

   _____

3. He can't never make that work.

   _____

4. The police wouldn't let no cars go into the lot.

   _____

5. This game doesn't never work properly.

   _____

6. My sister isn't never ready on time.

   _____

7. He didn't want no olives on his pizza.

   _____

8. Dad won't let no one use his camera again.

   _____

Extension: Write five (5) sentences using the contractions below.

can't   won't   isn't   didn't   weren't

Contractions
#5

I. Write contractions that fit the sentences on the lines below. Use the contractions in the box or make up your own.

she's	don't	you'll	can't	won't	I'm	aren't	it'll
hasn't	wouldn't	they'll	we've	he'll	didn't	we'll

1. Everyone said that ___**she's**___ the best singer.

2. They _____ ready to go yet.

3. Mom asked, "_____ it be nice if we all took a picture together?"

4. _____ need to get up early tomorrow.

5. _____ make any noise or _____ wake the baby.

6. Whenever _____ hungry I make a sandwich.

7. She _____ see so she is changing seats.

8. _____ be a long time before _____ argue with me again.

9. He told the teacher that he _____ make the mess.

10. Tina _____ help us clean the house.

11. We were ready to go, but Tim _____ put his shoes on.

12. _____ written many cards, and _____ deliver them tomorrow.

II. Turn the words below into contractions.

1. he will - _____**he'll**_____   6. I will - _____

2. they have - _____   7. they are - _____

3. will not - _____   8. cannot - _____

4. they would - _____   9. you are - _____

5. were not - _____   10. do not - _____

Contractions
#6

I. Write contractions that fit the sentences on the lines below. Use the contractions in the box or make up your own.

haven't don't shouldn't can't you'll aren't it's
we'll I'll isn't wouldn't you're won't hasn't

1. We promise that we _____ make fun of your new hair cut.

2. They _____ putting any candles on the birthday cake.

3. _____ make the beds if _____ clean the toilets.

4. She said that she _____ going to play.

5. Dad _____ clean the yard until he buys a new rake.

6. Kelly _____ let anyone touch her new necklace.

7. _____ we be in class right now?

8. _____ going to lose your place in line if you _____ come back.

9. If he _____ fixed the car by tomorrow, _____ walk to school.

10. _____ not a good idea to swim if you _____ taken lessons.

II. Rewrite the contractions below.

1. he'll - _____**he will**_____   6. there's - _____

2. they'd - _____   7. won't - _____

3. hasn't - _____   8. could've - _____

4. can't - _____   9. I'm - _____

5. don't - _____   10. weren't - _____

Extension: You lost your favorite toy. Write a story about how you found it. Use any five (5) contractions in your story.

Chapter 3
Review

I. Pronouns

Write the definition of a pronoun:

_____

Directions: Rewrite the sentences by changing the underlined nouns to pronouns.

1. <u>Lupe</u> gave a <u>present</u> to <u>Gena</u>.

    ____**She** gave **it** to **her**._____

2. <u>Dad</u> made <u>paper airplanes</u> for <u>Sammy and me</u>.

    _____

3. <u>The teachers</u> let the <u>students</u> have a <u>snack</u>.

    _____

4. <u>Amy</u> gave <u>Ben's</u> book to <u>John</u>.

    _____

5. <u>Marco and I</u> played checkers with our <u>friends</u>.

    _____

6. <u>Nancy and Carrie</u> borrowed <u>Cindy's</u> chairs for the <u>party</u>.

    _____

II. Verbs: Past, Present, and Future

Directions: Write the past, present, and future tense for the words below.

	Past Tense	Present Tense	Future Tense
1. sing -	_____	_____	_____
2. thought -	_____	_____	_____
3. read -	_____	_____	_____
4. will type -	_____	_____	_____
5. fight -	_____	_____	_____

III. Adjectives

A. Directions: Write three adjectives to describe each noun below.

1. puppy - _____ _____ _____

2. pizza - _____ _____ _____

3. mountains - _____ _____ _____

B. Directions: Change each adjective into a comparative and superlative.

Adjective	Comparative	Superlative
1. good	_____better_____	_____best_____
2. new	_____	_____
3. intelligent	_____	_____

IV. Contractions

A. Directions: Write the words below as a contraction.

1. cannot - _____   4. you are - _____

2. will not - _____   5. is not - _____

3. you have - _____   6. it is - _____

B. Fix each sentence below:

1. The camera didn't have no film in it.

   _____

2. We won't never get there.

   _____

Chapter 3
Test

I. Pronouns
Write the definition of a pronoun:

_____

Directions: Rewrite the sentences by changing the underlined nouns to pronouns.

1. <u>Mike</u> made a <u>card</u> for <u>his parents</u>.

   _____

2. <u>Mrs. Kim</u> found <u>the pencils</u> under <u>her folder</u>.

   _____

3. <u>Kim and Jocelyn</u> rode <u>bikes</u> with <u>Amy and me</u>.

   _____

4. <u>Joe and I</u> donated <u>money</u> for the fundraiser.

   _____

5. <u>The circus</u> showed <u>clowns</u> throwing pies at the <u>audience's</u> face.

   _____

II. Verbs: Past, Present, and Future
Directions: Write the past, present, and future tense for the words below.

	Past Tense	Present Tense	Future Tense
1. run -	_____	_____	_____
2. wrote -	_____	_____	_____
3. read -	_____	_____	_____
4. will help -	_____	_____	_____
5. learned -	_____	_____	_____

III. Adjectives

A. Directions: Write three adjectives to describe each noun below.

1. kitten - _____ _____ _____

2. ocean - _____ _____ _____

3. snake - _____ _____ _____

B. Directions: Fill in the blanks with the correct form of each word.

Adjective	Comparative	Superlative
1. good	_____	_____
2. old	_____	_____
3. famous	_____	_____

IV. Contractions

A. Directions: Write the words below as a contraction.

1. has not - _____   4. I am - _____

2. she is - _____   5. will not - _____

3. cannot - _____   6. we are - _____

B. Fix each sentence below:

1. The waiter didn't give us no napkins.

_____

2. She won't never leave.

_____

Chapter 3
Test - Answer Key

I. Pronouns

Write the definition of a pronoun:

_____**Pronouns take the place of a noun.**_____

Directions: Rewrite the sentences by changing the underlined nouns to pronouns.

1. <u>Mike</u> made a <u>card</u> for <u>his parents</u>.

   ___**He** made **it** for **them.**_____

2. <u>Mrs. Kim</u> found <u>the pencils</u> under <u>her folder</u>.

   ___**She** found **them** under **it.**_____

3. <u>Kim and Jocelyn</u> rode <u>bikes</u> with <u>Amy and me</u>.

   ___**They rode them with us.**_____

4. <u>Joe and I</u> donated <u>money</u> for the fundraiser.

   __**We** donated **it** for the fundraiser._____

5. <u>The circus</u> showed <u>clowns</u> throwing pies at the <u>audience's</u> face.

   __**It** showed **them** throwing pies at the **their** face._____

II. Verbs: Past, Present, and Future

Directions: Write the past, present, and future tense for the words below.

	Past Tense	Present Tense	Future Tense
1. run -	**ran**	**run**	**will run**
2. wrote -	**wrote**	**write**	**will write**
3. read -	**read**	**read**	**will read**
4. will help -	**helped**	**help**	**will help**
5. learned -	**learned**	**learn**	**will learn**

III. Adjectives

A. Directions: Write three adjectives to describe each noun below.

1. kitten – **Answers will vary**

2. ocean - **Answers will vary**

3. snake - **Answers will vary**

B. Directions: Fill in the blanks with the correct form of each word.

Adjective	Comparative	Superlative
1. good	**better**	**best**
2. old	**older**	**oldest**
3. famous	**more famous**	**most famous**

IV. Contractions

A. Directions: Write the words below as a contraction.

1. has not - **hasn't**   4. I am - **I'm**

2. she is - **she's**   5. will not - **won't**

3. cannot - **can't**   6. we are - **we're**

B. Fix each sentence below:

1. The waiter didn't give us no napkins.

The waiter didn't give us any napkins.

2. She won't never leave.

She won't ever leave. / or / She will never leave.

Unit 4

<u>Comma Rules</u>

Dates

City, State

Lists

Adjectives

Letters

_____

Student

Comma Rules

	Mastery	Non-Mastery
1. Dates		
2. City, State / Addresses		
3. Lists		
4. Adjectives		
5. Letters		

Grammar Standards – Unit 4

_____

Student

Comma Rules

	Mastery	Non-Mastery
1. Dates		
2. City, State / Addresses		
3. Lists		
4. Adjectives		
5. Letters		

Comma Rules
Dates
#1

What day were you born? If you say, "I was born on the 11ᵗʰ," you have left out an important piece of information - the month! Therefore, when you tell what day something happens, you need to include the month.

Rule #1: Day, Year -   January 1, 2008   June 30, 1775

* Do not put a comma
   after the month if no   January 2008   June 1775
   day is used.

- -

Directions: Place commas where they are needed. Next, rewrite the day and
year on the line below. * Watch out for months without a day.

A. March 3 2008   B. October 2007   C. December 25 2000

__**March 3, 2008**__   __**October 2007**__   _____

D. January 1 2010   E. April 8 1841   F. May 2005

_____   _____   _____

G. November 25 2002   H. February 2012   I. October 31 2007

_____   _____   _____

J. August 2004   K. December 31 1999   L. March 5 2005

_____   _____   _____

M. June 28 1824   N. May 18 2006   O. July 2015

_____   _____   _____

Comma Rules
Dates
#2

Name: _____

I. Place commas where they are needed. Next, rewrite the day and year on the line below. * Watch out for months without a day.

A. March 3 2008

__**March 3, 2008**__

B. October 2007

__**October 2007**__

C. December 25 2000

_____

D. June 27 2004

_____

E. September 1 1986

_____

F. February 1922

_____

G. August 2009

_____

H. January 4 2005

_____

I. March 9 2007

_____

J. April 30 1845

_____

K. May 1776

_____

L. July 4 1776

_____

II. Place commas in the story below where they are needed.

I was born on December 15 2000. My brother was born on January 16 2001, and my sister was born on February 17 2002. Can you guess when my dad was born? He was born on March 18 1973. My mom? She was born in April 1974, but she was born on the 6th. We all say that she spoiled the pattern. It would have been neat if she was born on the 14th or the 19th. At least the month fits the pattern. The funny thing is that our dog was born in May 2004 and our cat was born in June 2005. Another interesting fact is that my aunt had her baby on July 19 2005, and my uncle was born on August 20 1974. Does this mean anything? Maybe not, but it sure is weird.

Extension: Write each date below in a sentence. Be sure only to put commas where they are needed.

May 1 2007 / December 25 2010 / September 2008 / June 23 2009

Comma Rules
City, State / Addresses
#1

Rule #2: City, State – Place a **comma (,)** between the city and state.

 Examples: Phoenix**,** Arizona   Lakewood, California

Rule #3: Address – Use a **comma** after the street address, the city, and the state.

 Example: 555 Flower Street, Bellflower, California
                street address   **city**   **state**

— · — · — — · — — · — — · — — — · — — · — — · — — — · — — · — — · — — · — — · · —

I. Place commas where they are needed. Next, rewrite the city, state or address on the line below.

A. Los Angeles California

 Los Angeles, California

B. 321 Main Street Orange Florida

 321 Main Street, Orange, Florida

C. 11408 E. 211ᵗʰ Tulane OH

_____

D. Miami Florida

_____

E. Sacramento California

_____

F. 241 Jersey Way Denver Colorado

_____

G. 949 Arbor St. Franklin TN

_____

H. Houston Texas

_____

I. Portland Oregon

_____

J. 3305 Lees Ave. Atlanta Georgia

_____

K. 13 Big St. Kona Hawaii

_____

L. Las Vegas Nevada

_____

Comma Rules
City, State / Addresses
#2

I. Place commas where they are needed. Next, rewrite the city, state or address on the line below.

A. Boise Idaho

_____**Boise, Idaho**_____

B. 14732 Bowling Lane   Chicago Illinois

14732 Bowling Lane, Chicago, Illinois

C. 484 East St. Augusta Maine

_____

D. Minneapolis Minnesota

_____

E. Lincoln Nebraska

_____

F. 15243 West Point Albany New York

_____

G. 9185 Main Ave. Toledo OH

_____

H. Hershey Pennsylvania

_____

I. Salt Lake City Utah

_____

J. 22448 Kite St. Helena Montana

_____

II. Place commas in the story below where they are needed.

This summer my family is going to Springfield Missouri to visit my cousins. They just bought a new house. Their address is 327 Viking Way Galloway Missouri. It's just south of Springfield. On our way we hope to visit Flagstaff Arizona and see the Grand Canyon. We would also like to stop in San Antonio Texas to see the Alamo. While I'm gone I'm sending postcards to my friend Amy who lives at 323 Heart St. Bellflower California. I'll also send one to my grandma who lives on 4545 Henrilee Ave. Lawton Oklahoma.

Extension: How many cities and states can you name? Use a map to help you find five (5) cities from five (5) different states. List all five cities and their states. Be sure to put a comma between the city and state.

Example: Miami, Florida

Comma Rules
Dates / City, State / Addresses
Mixed Review

Name: _____

I. Place commas where they are needed. * Watch out for months without a day.

1. On April 22 2004 we went to Honolulu Hawaii.

2. Vacation started early in June 2003.

3. The contest said the letter arrived on April 5 2003 at 4531 E. Arlington Rd. Dallas Texas.

4. On May 3 1920 a plane made it from San Diego CA to Long Island New York.

5. Our family moved to 222 Washington Rd. Seal Beach CA in November 1988.

6. Santa lives at 123 Gum Drop Lane North Pole Alaska, I think.

7. In June 2006 the Olympic committee announced that the Olympics would be in Atlanta Georgia, and they will begin on February 2 2010.

8. The best time to visit our cabin at 396 Big Bear Ave. Arrowhead CA would be in July 2006

II. Write each item below in a sentence. Put commas where they are needed.

1. October 31 2010 - _____

_____

2. Brooklyn New York - _____

_____

3. 1314 Love Ave. Lakewood Colorado - _____

_____

4. June 2012 - _____

_____

5. August 12 2008 - _____

_____

6. 555 Hope Ave. Little Rock Arkansas - _____

_____

Comma Rules
Lists
#1

Rule #4: Lists

Use **commas (,)** to separate three or more items in a list. Do not put a comma after the last item in the list.

       Examples:

Mom bought me some <u>pencils, crayons, paper, and glue</u> for school.

Alyssa gave a Valentine's Day card to <u>Shawn, Ryan, and Tim.</u>

Directions: Put **commas (,)** after items in a list. Use a crayon to highlight the list.

1. We learned about the moon stars and planets in science.

2. There are scissors crayons and pencils on your table.

3. It seems like we read write and study all day.

4. Amy Sally and Melissa are best friends.

5. Mom told me to wash rinse and dry the dishes.

6. The store was out of chocolate vanilla and strawberry ice cream.

7. Our new puppy has chewed up my slippers socks dolls and homework.

8. We put milk butter sugar and flour into the recipe.

9. David Joy Shawna and Ryan are on the same team.

10. My mom's favorite holidays are Christmas Easter 4th of July and Thanksgiving.

11. We need to put spoons knives and forks on the table.

12. Leaves twigs and trash blew onto our yard.

13. Johnny has a fish dog mouse and lizard for a pet.

14. The show will start when the teachers students and parents enter.

15. Our team needs a new pitcher catcher and captain.

Comma Rules
Lists
#2

I. Place commas where they are needed. Use a crayon to highlight the list.

1. The story was about how a bird mouse and snake became friends.

2. The sun causes wind rain hurricanes and tornadoes.

3. Police fire-fighters and paramedics participated in the assembly.

4. We need glue scissors and tissue for our art project.

5. Washington Adams and Jefferson were our first presidents.

6. My dad is afraid of snakes spiders and mice.

7. Today I wrote revised and edited my report.

8. Her baby brother likes to be tickled on his belly feet and chin.

9. Mr. Alexander taught us about health science and history.

10. Along the beach were sand castles children and seaweed.

II. Write the items below in a sentence. Be sure to use them as a list, and place commas where they are needed.

1. (pizza / popcorn / soda)

   _____

2. (movies / video games / sports)

   _____

3. (Molly / Mary / Linda)

   _____

4. (rabbit / squirrel / skunk)

   _____

5. (walk / jog / sprint / run)

   _____

Comma Rules
Lists
#3

Directions: Write the items below in a sentence. Be sure to use them as a list, and place commas where they are needed. You may use "and" or "or" to connect the words.

1. (computer / television / VCR)

   _____

2. (field trip / assembly / party)

   _____

3. (pencil / paper / eraser)

   _____

4. (friends / neighbors / relatives)

   _____

5. (cake / ice cream / popcorn)

   _____

6. (potatoes / corn / turkey)

   _____

7. (soccer / tennis / football)

   _____

8. (flower / tree / plant)

   _____

Extension: Write five (5) sentences about things you use in each room of your house. Be sure to use items in a list in each sentence.

Comma Rules
Adjectives
#1

Rule #5: Adjectives

When you put more than one adjective in front of a noun, you need to put **commas (,)** to separate the list of adjectives.

Examples:

1. There was a <u>soft, cute, furry puppy</u> in the window of the store.

2. I love to eat <u>smooth, creamy peanut</u> butter.

Look at Example #2. What is the difference between putting a comma in "Items in a List" and "Adjectives"?

Answer: There needs to be three (3) items in a list before you can use commas. However, you need to place a comma even if there are only two adjectives before a noun. Also, there is no "and."

—··—··—··—··—··—··—··—··—··—··—··—··—··—··

Directions: Put **commas (,)** between the adjectives. Use a crayon to highlight the adjectives and the words they describe.

1. There were many bright colorful lights around the tree.

2. The strong brave workers saved the girl from the burning building.

3. We walked into the room and saw short busy elves making toys.

4. All the girls were wearing long clean colorful dresses.

5. The whining complaining children were ready for a nap.

6. We used our tongues to lick the sweet sticky syrup from our mouths.

7. The clown's thick curly colorful hair made him look funny.

8. Amy has small fuzzy animals all over her bed.

9. Many hungry dirty lumberjacks came into the restaurant.

10. Captain Hook was a mean nasty cheating no-good worthless pirate.

Comma Rules
Adjectives
#2

I. Put **commas (,)** between the adjectives. Use a crayon to highlight the adjectives and the words they describe.

1. We worked for two long hard hours on this puzzle.

2. Our new neighbors have two nice cheerful children.

3. Mom said it was time to throw away these old dirty shirts.

4. The dark flat clouds made their way across the sky.

5. Her tiny broken umbrella couldn't keep the cold sharp rain away.

6. The young handsome soldiers marched in the parade.

7. The song had a fun bouncy sound to it.

8. Yvette has such long dark beautiful hair.

9. The long boring game seemed to last forever.

10. The wild crazy boys destroyed the room.

Directions: Write the adjectives and nouns below in a sentence. Be sure to place commas where they are needed.

1. (cold hard floor)

   _____

2. (big heavy shelf)

   _____

3. (quick slippery lizard)

   _____

4. (soft smooth blanket)

   _____

5. (long wooden fence)

   _____

Comma Rules
Adjectives
#3

Directions: Write the adjectives and nouns below in a sentence. Be sure to place commas where they are needed.

1. (soft comfortable chair)

_____

2. (rich famous movie star)

_____

3. (plump jolly baby)

_____

4. (delicious healthy snack)

_____

5. (fun silly clown)

_____

6. (cool refreshing water)

_____

7. (big round bubble)

_____

8. (long thin tail)

_____

Extension: Use the list of adjectives below to write five (5) sentences about a circus. Use two or three adjectives to describe something in each sentence. Put the adjectives in front of the word they describe. Be sure to put commas where they are needed.

Adjectives

funny   big   floppy   bouncy   fast   crunchy   delicious

colorful   exciting   thrilling   dangerous   happy   smiling

short   fat   crazy   graceful   brave   skillful

* Use any other adjectives that come to mind.

Comma Rules
Friendly Letter
#1

Rule #6: Greeting

Place a **comma (,)** after the greeting in a friendly letter.

Examples:

    Dear Maria,   Dear Jose,   Dear Arthur,

Rule #7: Closing

Place a **comma (,)** after the closing in a friendly letter.

Examples:

    Yours truly,   Sincerely,   Friends forever,

Directions: Put **commas (,)** after the greeting and closing in the letters below. Write the word "Greeting" next to the greeting and "Closing" next to the closing.

1. Dear Nemo,   **Greeting**

    Stay there. Your dad is on his way.

                Sincerely,   **Closing**

                Dori

2. Dear Shrek

    See you at the swamp. I'll make the waffles.

                Your friend

                Donkey

3. Dear Belle

    Did you like the book <u>Where the Wild Things Are</u>?

                Truly yours

                Beast

4. Dear Woody

    Remember when you pushed me out of the window?

                Best wishes

                Buzz

5. Dear Sulley

    Don't forget to return Boo to her house today.

                Your friend

                Mike

Comma Rules
Friendly Letter
#2

I. Put **commas (,)** after the greeting and closing in the letters below. Write the word "Greeting" next to the greeting and "Closing" next to the closing.

1. Dear Mrs. Clause   _____
      Please send Rudolf. There's heavy fog tonight.
           Sincerely   _____
           Dasher

2. Dear Captain Hook   _____
      Sorry about the hand. Say hi to Crock for me.
           Your friend   _____
           Peter

3. Dear Pumbaa   _____
      How about cutting down on the beans?
           Your buddy   _____
           Timon

II. Write one-sentence letters to your friends. Use the lines below to help you place the greeting, body, closing, and signature in the correct place. Don't forget to place commas where they are needed.

1. _____

        _____

                              _____

                              _____

2. _____

        _____

                              _____

                              _____

Comma Rules
Friendly Letter
#3

Directions: Write one-sentence letters to your friends. Tell your friend something that you like about him or her. Use the lines below to help you place the greeting, body, closing, and signature in the correct place. Don't forget to place commas where they are needed.

1. _____

_____

_____

2. _____

_____

_____

3. _____

_____

_____

4. _____

_____

_____

_____

___

Extension: Pretend that you are any cartoon character. Write three (3) friendly letters to any other cartoon characters. Each letter only needs to be one or two sentences. Be sure to put commas where they are needed.

Comma Rules Mixed Review #1

Rule #1: Day, Year **Rule #4: Lists** **Rule #6: Greeting**

Rule #2: City, State **Rule #5: Adjectives** **Rule #7: Closing**

Rule #3: Address

I. Place commas where they are needed. Write the name of the rule below each comma.

1. There was a wild**,** exciting party on January 1**,** 2004.
   Adjectives   **Day, Year**

2. San Francisco California is famous for earthquakes hills houses and bridges.

3. Dear Porky

    In April 2012 meet me outside your house with a bottle of ketchup.

                                                Your friend

                                                B.B. Wolf

4. A soft cuddly bunny will enjoy a carrot radish or lettuce.

5. Williamsburg Virginia was a big crowded city on July 4 1776.

6. Dear Mickey

    You have the cutest large round ears.

                                                Sincerely

                                                Minnie

7. On May 19 1968 the moon earth and sun lined up.

8. A large hairy spider was found at 222 W. Palm Dr. in Miami Florida.

Extension: Write a sentence about each family member. Tell where they were born (city, state) and when they were born (day, year).

  Example: My dad was born in Spokane, Washington on August 15, 1971.

* Note: If your parents were born in a different country, write about the day they arrived in the United States.

Comma Rules
Mixed Review
#2

Rule #1: Day, Year   **Rule #4: Lists**   **Rule #6: Greeting**

Rule #2: City, State   **Rule #5: Adjectives**   **Rule #7: Closing**

Rule #3: Address

I. Place commas where they are needed. Write the name of the rule below each comma.

1. My dad proposed to my mom in Lincoln Nebraska on February 14 2000.

2. Dear Martha

   The soldiers just loved the biscuits gravy and jam.

   Love

   George W.

3. There was a concert in Denver Colorado in December 2001.

4. Mail the coupon to 293 Broadway Mobile Alabama for a free prize picture and autograph.

5. The fastest strongest wolf usually becomes the leader of the pack.

6. Dear Thomas

   My new address is 484 Eastern St. Brain Tree Massachusetts.

   Sincerely

   John

7. The silly entertaining clown wore a funny hat shoes and pants.

8. Parents can send post cards presents and treats to their children at 11934 Pine Ave. Crestline California.

Extension: Find the address of five friends or relatives. Write them each in a sentence. Be sure to use commas correctly.

Comma Rules
Mixed Review
#3

Rule #1: Day, Year   **Rule #4: Lists**   **Rule #6: Greeting**

Rule #2: City, State   **Rule #5: Adjectives**   **Rule #7: Closing**

Rule #3: Address

I. Place commas where they are needed. Write the name of the rule below each comma.

1. The address on the birthday invitation said 427 Stevely Branson Iowa.

2. She had cookies cake and ice cream at her party.

3. Old cartoons ended in December 2004, but started again on January 3 2004.

4. This summer we're going to St. Louis Missouri.

5. Mom put a large fluffy pancake on my plate.

6. Dear Rabbit

    You have such a beautiful peaceful garden.

              Yours truly

              Pooh

7. We love to run jump and slide in the snow.

8. My first house was 724 Ram St. Tulsa Oklahoma.

9. Is the happiest place on earth Anaheim California or Orlando Florida.

10. The Super Bowl was on February 6 2005

Extension:

1. Think about three (3) people you know. Write a birthday wish list for each person. Use commas in your lists.

    Example: Amy wants a doll, clothes, and a puppy.

2. Write three (3) sentences about things you want for your birthday. Use two adjectives before each noun.

    Example: I want a cute, cuddly puppy.

Comma Rules
Mixed Review
#4

Rule #1: Day, Year **Rule #4: Lists** **Rule #6: Greeting**

Rule #2: City, State **Rule #5: Adjectives** **Rule #7: Closing**

Rule #3: Address

I. Place commas where they are needed. Write the name of the rule below each comma.

1. The beautiful ancient tradition of Chanukah began on December 8 2004.

2. The furniture clothes and dishes will be delivered to 374 Main St Richmond Virginia.

3. Dear Ariel

   Do you give singing lessons? You have such an amazing angelic voice.

   Sincerely yours

   E. Fudd

4. There were floats bands and horses at the New Year's Day Parade on January 1 2003.

5. Brilliant hard-working scientists predict that there will be a colony on Mars by December 2050.

6. Dear Mr. Troll

   Sorry about that whole bridge thing. I hope your head feels better.

   Yours truly

   Bill Goat

Extension: Think of any three (3) characters from any stories that you have read. Write three (3) letters, one or two sentences long, that these characters might write to someone else in their story.

For example, in <u>Charlotte's Web</u>, Wilbur might write a letter to Charlotte, thanking her for her help.

Be sure to use commas in your greeting and closing.

Comma Rules
Test

Rule #1: Day, Year   **Rule #4: Lists**   **Rule #6: Greeting**
Rule #2: City, State   **Rule #5: Adjectives**   **Rule #7: Closing**
Rule #3: Address

I. Place commas where they are needed.

1. In May 1905 there was a giant earthquake in San Francisco California.

2. Send the package to 374 W. Elm St. Boston Massachusetts.

3. Dear Rosa

    You were the most beautiful talented dancer in the show.

    Sincerely
    Mandy

4. The winner of the lottery lives at 333 Walker Rd. Lincoln Nebraska.

5. After the storm there were branches leaves and trash piled everywhere.

6. She was born on September 9 1975.

7. We are going to replace our old dry grass with new fresh grass.

8. We saw so many fish birds and elephants at the zoo.

9. Debbie moved to Austin Texas.

10. Bobby's new address is 12499 North Ave. Phoenix Arizona.

11. Some think that the war started in Jan. 1942, but it started on Dec. 7 1941.

12. Dear Santa

    Please send me a bike football and Easy Bake Oven. Please don't tell anyone about the Easy Bake Oven.

    Yours truly
    Jack

13. After a hard day of work we loved our soft comfortable beds.

14. The party was on July 4 2004.

15. Be sure to send the package to 12 Karen Ave. Torrance California.

16. In July 2005 Mrs. Ferguson went to Madison Wisconsin.

Comma Rule
Checklist

Directions: Below is a record of the comma rules that you passed. If you did not answer all questions correctly for each comma rule, your teacher will ask you to write sentences to practice the rules you missed. Your teacher might even let you retake the comma rules test when you finish to try to improve your grade.

Comma Rules	Pass	Needs Work
Rule #1 Day, Year *Questions: #6, #10, #14*		
Rule #2 City, State *Questions: #1, #9, #16*		
Rule #3 Address *Questions: #4, #10, #15*		
Rule #4 Lists *Questions: #5, #8, #12*		
Rule #5 Adjectives *Questions: #3, #7, #13*		
Rule #6 Greetings *Questions: #3 , #12,*		
Rule #7 Closing *Questions: #3, #12,*		

Unit 5

Four Types of Sentences

Subjects and Predicates

Finding Subjects and Predicates

_____

Student

	Mastery	Non-Mastery
1. Four Types of Sentences		
2. Subjects and Predicates		
3. Finding Subjects and Predicates		

Grammar Standards – Unit 5

_____

Student

	Mastery	Non-Mastery
1. Four Types of Sentences		
2. Subjects and Predicates		
3. Finding Subjects and Predicates		

Four Types of Sentences
#1

Name: _____

1. **Declarative Sentence**: This type of sentence states a fact. It ends with a period. (**.**)

Examples:

The movie starts at eight o'clock**.**

Once upon a time there were three bea**rs.**

The Trick: Think of a Southern belle. A Southern belle is a very proper young woman. Draw a picture of her saying, " I declare! I am making a declarative sentence."

[box: **Declarative Sentence**]

2. **Interrogative Sentence:** This type of sentence asks a question. It ends with a question mark. (**?**)

Examples:

Where are you going **?**
Who is the best player on the team**?**

The Trick: When the police ask a suspected criminal some questions, they are "interrogating" him. Draw a picture of a police officer interrogating, or questioning, a prisoner under two hot lights.

[box: **Interrogative Sentence**]

Directions: If the sentence is declarative, write "Declarative". If the sentence is interrogative, write "Interrogative". Put a period or question mark at the end.

_____ 1. Where are you going____

_____ 2. I'm going to the store____

_____ 3. There's a sale on shirts____

_____ 4. How much are the shirts____

_____ 5. You can get two shirts for fifteen dollars____

Four Types of Sentences
#2

What is a declarative sentence? _____

What is an interrogative sentence? _____

I. If the sentence is declarative, write "Declarative". If the sentence is interrogative, write "Interrogative". Put a period or question mark at the end.

_____ 1. The male emperor penguin sits on the egg____

_____ 2. How long does it take for the egg to hatch____

_____ 3. The egg rests on the penguin's toes for sixty-five days____

_____ 4. The mother leaves to feed in the ocean____

_____ 5. Will the mother penguin return____

_____ 6. Suzie asked, "When will the father penguin eat____"

_____ 7. Many penguins bunch together to stay warm____

_____ 8. Warm penguins on the inside let the outside penguins

come to the center____

_____ 9. Can the emperor penguin fly____

_____ 10. These penguins can't fly, but they are great swimmers ____

II. Pretend that there was an argument at school. The teacher is trying to figure out what happened. Write interrogative sentences a teacher might ask. Next, write declarative statements a student might say in response.

1. Interrogative: _____

   Declarative: _____

2. Interrogative: _____

   Declarative: _____

3. Interrogative: _____

   Declarative: _____

4. Interrogative: _____

   Declarative: _____

Four Types of Sentences
#3

Exclamatory Sentence

1. **Exclamatory Sentence**: This type of sentence states strong feeling or emotion. It ends with an exclamation point. (!)

Examples:

Hurry! The movie starts in ten minutes !

Watch out for that car !

The Trick: Draw a picture of someone kicking the winning goal at a soccer game. Write: "We're champions !" exclaimed Jose.

2. **Imperative Sentence**: This type of sentence gives a command or makes a request. It ends with a period. (.)

Examples:

Wait for me.
Please put that on the table.

The Trick: Draw two people having a conversation. One person says, "Tell me what an imperative is." The other person says, "You just said an imperative." The first person says, "Tell me what I said." The other responds, " You just did it again."

Imperative Sentence

Directions: If the sentence is exclamatory, write "Exclamatory". If the sentence is imperative, write "Imperative". Put a period or exclamation point at the end.

_____ 1. Watch your step____

_____ 2. The house is on fire____

_____ 3. The British are coming____

_____ 4. Please save a piece for me____

_____ 5. Take out a piece of paper____

Four Types of Sentences
#4

Name: _____

What is an exclamatory sentence? _____

What is an imperative sentence? _____

I. If the sentence is exclamatory, write "Exclamatory." If the sentence is imperative, write "Imperative." Put a period or exclamation point at the end.

_____ 1. The crowd shouted, "We're not going to take it anymore____"

_____ 2. Make your bed before you go to school____

_____ 3. We just won a million dollars____

_____ 4. Stop bothering your brother____

_____ 5. Wait for me outside your school____

_____ 6. I need a doctor in here, now____

_____ 7. "They're going to be late if we don't hurry____" screamed Amy.

_____ 8. Hurry up please____

_____ 9. Finish your homework when you get home from school____

_____ 10. The water is overflowing out of the tub____

II. There's a fire and some fire fighters are working hard. Write three (3) exclamatory sentences that someone might say at the fire. Next, write three (3) imperative sentences the chief fire fighter might say.

Exclamatory Sentences

1. _____

2. _____

3. _____

Imperative Sentences

1. _____

2. _____

3. _____

Four Types of Sentences
#5

What is an interrogative sentence? _____

What is an imperative sentence? _____

I. Write Declarative, Interrogative, Exclamatory, or Imperative next to each
   sentence. Put a period, exclamation point, or question mark at the end.

_____ 1. Don't killer whales hunt together in packs____

_____ 2. Killer whales will eat walruses, seals, and sea turtles____

_____ 3. "I see a killer whale____" shouted the ship's captain.

_____ 4. Listen to the sound the whale makes____

_____ 5. Jenny yelled excitedly, "The whale just caught a fish____"

_____ 6. How do killer whales trap and eat land animals____

_____ 7. Killer whales use their tails to splash animals into the water____

_____ 8. "Killer whales are cool____" shouted Tommy.

_____ 9. Look at the white spot around the whale's eye____

_____ 10. These whales swallow their food whole without chewing____

_____ 11. Aren't killer whales also called orcas____

II. Write four (4) exclamatory sentences that a rescue worker would say after an
    earthquake. End each sentence with "exclaimed the worker."

   Example: "If you're homeless, go to the shelter!" exclaimed the worker.

1. _____

   _____

2. _____

   _____

3. _____

   _____

4. _____

   _____

Four Types of Sentences
#6

What is a declarative sentence? _____

What is an exclamatory sentence? _____

I. Directions: Write Declarative, Interrogative, Exclamatory, or Imperative next to each sentence. Put a period, exclamation point, or question mark at the end.

_____ 1. Listen to these facts about koalas____

_____ 2. Koalas are marsupials and carry their babies in pouches____

_____ 3. "The baby koala is so cute____" exclaimed Nancy.

_____ 4. How old are baby koalas when they leave the pouch____

_____ 5. Look how the koala eats the eucalyptus leaves____

_____ 6. After seven months, the koala is old enough to leave the pouch____

_____ 7. Read more about koalas at your library____

_____ 8. Newborn koalas are the size of a jellybean____

_____ 9. What is a koala's favorite food____

_____ 10. "We need to protect the koalas____" shouted the protesters.

_____ 11. A shocked Paul yelled, "That koala just jumped to another tree___"

_____ 12. Where did you learn so much about koalas____

II. Write four (4) imperative sentences that a teacher might say.

   Example: "Put your homework in the basket" requested the teacher.

   1. _____

   _____

   2. _____

   _____

   3. _____

   _____

   4. _____

   _____

Subjects and Predicates

For the Teacher:

For many third graders, thinking about subjects and predicates is a new way of looking at sentences. Before doing any of these worksheets, the teacher needs to go over the definitions of subjects (the who or what of the sentence) and predicates (what the subject is or does). Once they understand the definitions, the worksheets will give them examples of subjects and predicates in action. By finding subjects and predicates within simple sentences, the students will be ready to write more complex sentences without the fear of creating run-ons.

Introduce the Idea:

Part I – The Subject

1. Write a short sentence on the board or on sentence strips.
2. Ask the students to find the subject of the sentence.
3. Add adjectives and prepositional phrases to the sentence. Ask the students if the subject has changed.
4. Put phrases in front of the sentence. Ask the students if the subject is the same.
5. Review the definition of a subject:
    a. Have the students say "subject" five times.
    b. Chant: "Who or what the sentence is about."

Example A for the students:

1. The dog barked.

2. Subject = dog

3. The big, ugly dog barked at the mailman.   The subject is still "dog".

4. In the front yard the big, ugly dog barked at the mailman.   The subject is still "dog".

5. "Dog" is always the who or what of the sentence.

Example B for the students:

1. The dress is pretty.

2. Subject = dress

3. The dress in the window is pretty.   The subject is still "dress".

4. The pink flowery dress in the window is pretty.   The subject is still "dog".

5. "Dress" is always the what of the sentence.

* Now, do Subject Worksheets #1 - #3

Part II – The Predicate

Repeat steps #1- #5 again. This time focus on the predicate. Now that the students know the subject, they can figure out what the subject is or does.

1. Write a short sentence on the board or on sentence strips.

2. Ask the students to find the predicate of the sentence.

3. Add adjectives and prepositional phrases to the sentence. Ask the students if the predicate has changed.

4. Put phrases in front of the sentence. Ask the students if the predicate is the same.

5. Review the definition of a predicate:

    a. Have the students say "predicate" five times.

    b. Chant: "What the subject is or does."

Example A for the students:

1. The dog barked.

2. Predicate = barked

3. The big, ugly dog barked at the mailman.   The predicate is still "barked".

4. In the front yard the big, ugly dog barked at the mailman.   The predicate is still "barked".

5. "Barked" is always what the subject does.

Example B for the students:

1. The dress is pretty.

2. Predicate = is pretty

3. The dress in the window is pretty.   The predicate is still "is pretty".

4. The pink flowery dress in the window is pretty.   The predicate is still "is pretty".

5. "Is pretty" is always the "is" of the sentence.

* Now, do Predicate Worksheets #1 - #3

Subjects
#1

Subject: The who or what of the sentence.

To find the subject of any sentence, ask yourself, "What is the who or what of the sentence?"

Example: **The bird flew away.**

Who or what is this sentence about?   Bird

When the cat came around, the bird flew away.

Is the subject cat or bird? Remember, this sentence is still about the bird. It is about what the bird did when the cat came around. Therefore, the subject is still "bird".

I. Subjects: Who or What?

Directions: Is each subject below a who or a what? Write "who" or "what" next to each word.

_____ 1. Mrs. Garcia   _____ 6. they

_____ 2. ice   _____ 7. hammer

_____ 3. (it)   _____ 8. button

_____ 4. student   _____ 9. singer

_____ 5. trees   _____ 10. tractor

II. Find the Subject

Directions: Write the subject of each sentence on the line.

_____ 1. Mrs. Garcia is my teacher.

_____ 2. The pencil belongs to Mrs. Garcia.

_____ 3. The ice is melting in the sun.

_____ 4. A girl needs ice for her drink.

_____ 5. Our tree loses most of its leaves in December.

_____ 6. A bird fell out of the tree.

_____ 7. Dad used a hammer to fix the fence.

_____ 8. The hammer fell on my foot.

_____ 9. A button came off of my shirt.

_____ 10. Mom sewed the button back on my shirt.

Subjects
#2

The subject is the _____ or _____ of the sentence.

I. Subjects: Who or What?

Directions: Is each subject below a who or a what? Write "who" or "what" next to each word.

_____ 1. bird   _____ 6. love

_____ 2. friend   _____ 7. photographer

_____ 3. pencil   _____ 8. helper

_____ 4. teacher   _____ 9. paper

_____ 5. parent   _____ 10. idea

II. Circle the subject in each sentence. If the subject is a "who," write "who" on the line. If the subject is a "what," write "what" on the line.

1. The radio played music all night.   _____

2. Music played on the radio all night.   _____

3. After the concert Mr. Jones smiled.   _____

4. The concert was enjoyed by Mr. Jones.   _____

5. A big, mean, angry wrestler threw a chair into the crowd.

   _____

6. The crowd threw the chair back at the wrestler.   _____

7. Love can solve so many problems.   _____

8. The room was filled with a lot of love.   _____

9. The paper fell onto the floor.   _____

10. You need to write your name on the paper.   _____

Name: _____

Subjects
#3

What is a subject? _____

I. Subjects: Who or What?
   Directions: Is each subject below a who or a what? Write "who" or "what"
     next to each word.

_____ 1. he   _____ 6. dollar

_____ 2. fork   _____ 7. leader

_____ 3. doll   _____ 8. memory

_____ 4. it   _____ 9. music

_____ 5. sailor   _____ 10. farmer

II. Circle the subject in each sentence. If the subject is a "who," write "who"
   on the line. If the subject is a "what," write "what" on the line.

1. He told him about the party. _____

2. A party would be a lot of fun. _____

3. The fork fell onto the floor. _____

4. It needed to be cleaned. _____

5. A cute, little doll rested on the bed. _____

6. The bed had a cute little doll on it. _____

7. Only a dollar is needed to ride on the train. _____

8. The ride only costs a dollar. _____

9. Her memory is very good. _____

10. Jay has a very good memory. _____

Extension: Write five (5) sentences using the words below as subjects.
Underline the word in your sentence.

    Example: The <u>water</u> spilled on the floor.

    water   **coach**   **book**   **friend**   **game**

Predicates
#1

Name: _____

Predicate: What the subject is or does.

To find the predicate of any sentence, ask yourself, "What is the subject doing?" or "Is the subject something?"

Example #1: **The bird flew away.**

What did the bird do?   It "flew away"

When the cat came around, the bird flew away.

What did the bird do? It "flew away when the cat came around"

Example #2: **The children are happy.**

Are the children doing anything? No.

Are the children something? Yes, they "are happy".

Remember: If you see the words "is, are, was, were, or am", then the predicate is explaining what the subject IS.

Directions: 1. Circle the subject in each sentence. 2. Underline the predicate in each sentence. 3. Write "Is" on the line if the predicate explains what the subject is. Write "Does" if the predicate explains what the subject does.

Examples:

___Does___   The bird flew away when the cat came around.

___Does___   When the cat came around, the bird flew away.

Is or Does?   **(Be sure to ask, "What did the subject do?)**

___**Is**___   1. Mrs. Garcia is my teacher at Elliot School.

_____   2. At Elliot School, Mrs. Garcia is my teacher.

_____   3. Our tree is bare in December.

_____   4. In December our tree is bare.

_____   5. After school, the teacher gave us a pencil.

_____   6. The teacher gave us a pencil after school.

_____   7. During recess, leaves were everywhere.

_____   8. Leaves were everywhere during recess.

Predicates
#2

Simple and Complete Predicates

The **predicate** tells what the subject is or does.

The **complete predicate** tells everything the subject is or does.

The **simple predicate** is the main verb or verb phrase that tells what the subject is or does.

Examples:

The dog is barking at the mailman.

Subject = dog   **Complete Predicate** = is barking at the mailman

Simple Predicate = is barking

Directions: Underline the complete predicate in each sentence. Circle the simple predicate. Write "Is" on the line if the predicate explains what the subject is. Write "Does" if the predicate explains what the subject does.

Example: __**Does**__ Amy dropped the penny into the fountain.

Is or Does?   (Be sure to ask, "What did the subject do?)

_____ 1. We made caramel apples.

_____ 2. I am sorry about the broken glass.

_____ 3. The magnet pulled the nails across the table.

_____ 4. A puppy is hungry.

_____ 5. Some puppies played on the grass.

_____ 6. The bell rang at the end of recess.

_____ 7. Those students were leaders of student council.

_____ 8. Many people are good helpers during the holidays.

_____ 9. We are good workers.

_____ 10. The drivers found a safe place to park during the storm.

Name: _____

Predicates
#3

Directions: Circle the simple predicate in each sentence. Underline the complete predicate. Write "Is" on the line if the predicate explains what the subject is. Write "Does" if the predicate explains what the subject does.

Example: __**Does**__ Amy (dropped) the penny into the fountain.

Is or Does?   (Be sure to ask, "What did the subject do?)

_____ 1. Emily rode the pony all morning.

_____ 2. She is an expert rider.

_____ 3. Our old car broke down.

_____ 4. We are happy about walking to school.

_____ 5. The big brown truck drove down the street.

_____ 6. The parents are happy with their children.

_____ 7. A lion is king of the jungle.

_____ 8. Some boys threw small, rubber spiders in our laps.

_____ 9. The show was ready to start.

_____ 10. A purple dinosaur sang a song about friends.

_____ 11. The girls are winners of the game.

_____ 12. The boys were good sports.

Extension: Write three (3) sentences using the predicate as an "is" and three sentences (3) using the predicate as a does. Use the three words below as your subjects.

puppies   kittens   sharks

Example:
"Is" – Puppies are cute.
"Does" - Puppies love to nibble on your ears.

Finding
Subjects and Predicates
#1

What is a subject? _____

What is a predicate? _____

I. If the complete subject is underlined, write "subject" on the line. If the complete predicate is underlined, write "predicate" on the line.

Remember, ask yourself: "Who or what is the subject, and what did it do?"

__predicate__   1. After the rain, the clouds <u>went away</u>.

_____   2. <u>The dark clouds</u> came back the next day.

_____   3. Mary <u>drank all of the milk</u>.

_____   4. <u>A big bottle of orange juice</u> was still in the refrigerator.

_____   5. Dad <u>gave a large red rose to Mom</u>.

_____   6. <u>A wet, sloppy kiss</u> was planted on Dad's cheek.

_____   7. Our entire family <u>worked on a puzzle all day</u>.

_____   8. The silly puzzle <u>took three hours to build</u>.

_____   9. <u>Before school</u> we <u>finished our homework</u>.

_____   10. After recess <u>our wonderful teacher</u> gave us prizes.

II. Circle the simple subject and simple predicate in each sentence from Part I.

Finding
Subjects and Predicates
#2

I. If the complete subject is underlined, write "subject" on the line. If the complete predicate is underlined, write "predicate" on the line.

Remember, ask yourself: "Who or what is the subject, and what did it do?"

__**predicate**__　　1. <u>Before the concert</u> the director <u>gave a speech</u>.

_____　　2. <u>A strong wind</u> blew over our tent.

_____　　3. Linda <u>wore a beautiful, red sweater</u>.

_____　　4. A hungry lion <u>chased that zebra</u>.

_____　　5. <u>The shiny trophy on the table</u> will be given today.

_____　　6. The campers <u>built a campfire</u>.

_____　　7. <u>Several girls</u> roasted marsh mellows.

_____　　8. <u>A little squirrel</u> raced across the ground.

_____　　9. <u>At the lake</u> the boys <u>swung from tires into the water</u>.

_____　　10. After the concert <u>the audience</u> cheered loudly.

II. Circle the simple subject and simple predicate in each sentence in Part I.

Extension: Write five (5) sentences about a party. Circle the simple subject and simple predicate in each sentence.

Name: _____

Finding
Subjects and Predicates
#3

I. Finding the Subject and Predicate

Directions: Circle the simple subject. Underline the complete predicate.

Example: The (ball) rolled down the hill.
What   Does

1. The frog jumped into the water.

2. The fish is in the pond.

3. Some big, hairy spiders live under that rock.

4. I am tired of washing the dog.

5. A fly buzzed around my ear.

6. A cow was in the field.

7. Mother bears protect their cubs.

8. Turtle eggs hatch in the sand.

9. Many birds are wet because of the rain.

10. The lizard's tail broke off.

11. The toucan is yellow and red with orange feathers.

12. Several butterflies are on the grass.

II. Subjects = Who or What / Predicates = Is or Does

Directions: Look at the sentences in Part I. Write "who" or "what" below each subject. Write "is" or "does" below each predicate.

Finding
Subjects and Predicates
#4

I. Finding the Subject and Predicate

Directions: Circle the subject. Underline the complete predicate.

Example: The (ball) rolled down the hill.
          <small>What   Does</small>

1. Cheetahs are faster than zebras.

2. The silver fish glistened in the light.

3. A snake rested on a rock in the warm sun.

4. The clever mouse always tricks the cat.

5. Some hungry kittens waited for their mother.

6. A scarecrow in the field scared away the birds.

7. The silly turkey wants to fly.

8. Several horses galloped across the field.

9. A bull dog is strong.

10. Worms are good diggers.

11. A little lizard climbed the wall.

12. That big, bad dog ate my homework.

II. Subjects = Who or What / Predicates = Is or Does

Directions: Look at the sentences in Part I. Write "who" or "what" below each subject. Write "is" or "does" below each predicate.

> **Extension:** Below is a list of subjects. Add a predicate to each subject by explaining what the subject IS. Use "is, are, was, or were."
>
> 1. The teachers   2. The students   3. The parents
>
>   4. The playground   5. The homework

Chapter 5
Review #1

I. Four Types of Sentences

Directions: Write Declarative, Interrogative, Exclamatory, or Imperative next to each sentence. Put a period, exclamation point, or question mark at the end.

_____ 1. We dressed as pirates for the party____

_____ 2. Where did you get that beautiful dress____

_____ 3. Set the book over there____

_____ 4. "There's a bee on your head____" shouted Mary.

_____ 5. Ask the teacher for a pencil____

_____ 6. How many times do we need to read the letter____

_____ 7. Mom screamed, "I just won the lottery____"

_____ 8. Some say that cats have nine lives____

II. Subjects and Predicates

A. Subjects: Who or What?

Directions: Is each subject below a who or a what? Write "who" or "what" next to each word.

_____ 1. snow   _____ 5. reporter

_____ 2. doctor   _____ 6. desk

_____ 3. soldier   _____ 7. cane

_____ 4. street   _____ 8. president

B. **Directions**: Underline the complete predicate in each sentence. Write "Is" on the line if the predicate explains what the subject is. Write "Does" if the predicate explains what the subject does.

Is or Does?   **(Be sure to ask, "What did the subject do?)**

_____ 1. The Trojans are the champions.

_____ 2. A river flows across my grandpa's farm.

_____ 3. During recess children played on the swings.

_____ 4. We were tired after the game.

_____ 5. Rain drops fell on our heads.

III. Finding the Subject and Predicate

Directions: Circle the simple subject. Underline the complete predicate.

Example: The (ball) <u>rolled down the hill</u>.

1. Some red paint spilled out of the cup.

2. Flowers are in the garden.

3. Bats hang from the top of caves.

4. My dog barked at the cat for an hour.

5. Our class is the best.

6. Spiders spin beautiful webs.

7. Cindy drank all of the juice.

8. She was late for dinner.

Chapter 5
Review #2

Name: _____

I. Four Types of Sentences

Directions: Write Declarative, Interrogative, Exclamatory, or Imperative next to each sentence. Put a period, exclamation point, or question mark at the end.

_____ 1. Will I get a good grade on this test____

_____ 2. Put your sweater in the closet____

_____ 3. Carrie shouted, "There's a spider in my hair____"

_____ 4. We're going to the dentist tomorrow____

_____ 5. A tornado is coming____

_____ 6. What is your favorite candy____

_____ 7. Chocolate is my favorite____

_____ 8. Don't eat that candy until after dinner____

II. Subjects and Predicates

A. Subjects: Who or What?

Directions: Is each subject below a who or a what? Write "who" or "what" next to each word.

_____ 1. secretary   _____ 5. stapler

_____ 2. hospital   _____ 6. leader

_____ 3. lady   _____ 7. director

_____ 4. bread   _____ 8. pocket

B. **Directions**: Underline the complete predicate in each sentence. Write "Is" on the line if the predicate explains what the subject is. Write "Does" if the predicate explains what the subject does.

Is or Does?   **(Be sure to ask, "What did the subject do?)**

_____ 1. Many birds fly south for the winter.

_____ 2. My mom is a teacher.

_____ 3. The puppies were ready for a bone.

_____ 4. Happy children threw darts at the balloons.

_____ 5. Ants find food in the weirdest places.

III. Finding the Subject and Predicate

Directions: Circle the simple subject. Underline the complete predicate.

Example: The ball rolled down the hill.

1. Butterflies are hard to catch.
2. Our class reads the most books every month.
3. Ken is a born leader.
4. Bright, colorful flowers grow in our garden.
5. A strange sound came from the corner of the room.
6. My new doll talks to me.
7. We are best friends.
8. A funny clown sprayed water in someone's face.

Chapter 5
Test

I. Four Types of Sentences

Directions: Write Declarative, Interrogative, Exclamatory, or Imperative next to each sentence. Put a period, exclamation point, or question mark at the end.

_____ 1. Draw a picture of the story____

_____ 2. Where did you put your homework____

_____ 3. It's getting dark outside____

_____ 4. "Donna better leave me alone____", shouted Laura.

_____ 5. How did you make that picture____

_____ 6. The puppy is cute____

_____ 7. Wait here for the teacher____

_____ 8. We screamed, "We're the champions____"

II. Subjects and Predicates

A. Subjects: Who or What?

Directions: Is each subject below a who or a what? Write "who" or "what" next to each word.

_____ 1. doctor

_____ 2. farm

_____ 3. friend

_____ 4. ice

_____ 5. movie

_____ 6. builder

_____ 7. coach

_____ 8. ring

B. **Directions**: Underline the complete predicate in each sentence. Write "Is" on the line if the predicate explains what the subject is. Write "does" if the predicate explains what the subject does.

Is or Does?   **(Be sure to ask, "What did the subject do?")**

_____ 1. Some children read stories on the rug.

_____ 2. My friends are great buddies.

_____ 3. Her family was ready for their vacation.

_____ 4. Silly students played in the puddles.

_____ 5. Butterflies flew through the flowers.

III. Finding the Subject and Predicate

Directions: Circle the simple subject. Underline the complete predicate.

Example: The (ball) <u>rolled down the hill</u>.

1. Ryan won the contest.
2. A strong wind blew over our tent.
3. Sasha is the best singer.
4. A big, ugly spider made a web in my yard.
5. Small raindrops dropped on my head.
6. Her old sweater fits me.
7. They were strong swimmers.
8. A hungry seal begged for a fish.

Chapter 5
Test - Answer Key

I. Four Types of Sentences

__Imperative__   1. Draw a picture of the story.

__Interrogative__   2. Where did you put your homework?

__Declarative__   3. It's getting dark outside.

__Exclamatory__   4. "Donna better leave me alone!", shouted Laura.

__Interrogative__   5. How did you make that picture?

__Declarative__   6. The puppy is cute.

__Imperative__   7. Wait here for the teacher.

__Exclamatory__   8. We screamed, "We're the champions!"

II. Subjects and Predicates
A. Subjects: Who or What?

__Who__   1. doctor   __What__   5. movie

__What__   2. farm   __Who__   6. builder

__Who__   3. friend   __Who__   7. coach

__What__   4. ice   __What__   8. ring

B. Directions: Underline the complete predicate in each sentence. Write "Is" on the line if the predicate explains what the subject is. Write "Does" if the predicate explains what the subject does.

Is or Does?   (Be sure to ask, "What did the subject do?)

__does__   1. Some children <u>read stories on the rug</u>.

__is__   2. My friends <u>are great buddies</u>.

__is__   3. Her family <u>was ready for their vacation</u>.

__does__   4. Silly students <u>played in the puddles</u>.

__is__   5. Butterflies <u>flew through the flowers</u>.

III. Finding the Subject and Predicate

Directions: Circle the simple subject. Underline the complete predicate.

Example: The (ball) rolled down the hill.

1. (Ryan) won the contest.
2. A strong (wind) blew over our tent.
3. (Sasha) is the best singer.
4. A big, ugly (spider) made a web in my yard.
5. Small (raindrops) dropped on my head.
6. Her old (sweater) fits me.
7. (They) were strong swimmers.
8. A hungry (seal) begged for a fish.

Unit 6

Phrases

Fragment and Run-On Sentences

Titles or Topic Sentences

Subject-Verb Agreement

_____

Student

	Mastery	Non-Mastery
1. Phrases		
2. Fragment and Run-On Sentences		
3. Title or Topic Sentence		
4. Subject-Verb Agreement		

Grammar Standards – Unit 6

_____

Student

	Mastery	Non-Mastery
1. Phrases		
2. Fragment and Run-On Sentences		
3. Title or Topic Sentence		
4. Subject-Verb Agreement		

Name: _____

Phrases #1

A **sentence** tells a **complete thought**.

A **phrase** is a **group of words** that <u>help</u> tell the complete thought. Some students think that they are writing sentences when they are just writing phrases.

Two Types of Phrases

1. **Prepositional Phrase**: Begins with a preposition and ends with its object.

    Examples: <u>into</u> the <u>street</u>   <u>inside</u> the <u>room</u>
             Preposition Object   Preposition Object

I. Prepositional Phrases

Directions: The box shows some common prepositions. Write a preposition on the line that would complete the phrase. Use each preposition only once.

above	at	between	inside	out	under
across	before	by	into	outside	until
after	behind	for	of	over	up
against	below	from	on	through	with
around	beside	in	onto	to	without

1. _____ the room   7. _____ me   13. _____ the cloud

2. _____ the fence   8. _____ the hill   14. _____ the cloud

3. _____ my shoe   9. _____ Joe   15. _____ the cloud

4. _____ my shoe   10. _____ you   16. _____ the cloud

5. _____ my shoe   11. _____ the trees   17. _____ one o'clock

6. _____ my shoe   12. _____ school   18. _____ a pencil

Extension: Write each preposition below in a phrase.

   above   at   between   inside   out
   under   across   before   by   into

Phrases
#2

Name: _____

A **sentence** tells a **complete thought**.

A **phrase** is a **group of words** that <u>help</u> tell the complete thought. Some students think that they are writing sentences when they are just writing phrases.

Two Types of Phrases

2. **Verb Phrase:** A group of words which includes the helping verbs and the main verb.

Examples: <u>is</u> <u>running</u>   <u>will be</u> <u>running</u>

helping verb main verb   helping verbs main verb

I. Verb Phrases

Directions: The box shows some common helping verbs. Write a helping verb on the line that would complete the verb phrase. Use each helping verb only once.

Helping Verbs							
is	are	was	were	be	been	being	can
could	did	do	does	had	has	have	may
might	must	shall	should	will	would		

1. __is__ jumping   5. _____ been waiting   9. _____ sing

2. _____ smile   6. _____ be making   10. _____ call

3. _____ climbed   7. _____ walking   11. _____ written

4. _____ write   8. _____ have stopped   12. _____ make

Extension: Write five (5) sentences using any of the verb phrases from above.

Example: The car <u>should have stopped</u> at the light.

CreateBetterWriters.com   142

Phrases
#3

I. Directions: If the phrase below is a <u>prepositional phrase</u>, write "Prep" on the line. If the phrase is a <u>verb phrase</u>, write "Verb."

_____ 1. in the house

_____ 2. is swimming

_____ 3. without me

_____ 4. are jumping

_____ 5. through the cloud

_____ 6. inside the fence

_____ 7. will be drinking

_____ 8. for me

_____ 9. must play

_____ 10. did walk

II. Underline all of the phrases in each sentence. Below the phrase, write "Prep" if it is a prepositional phrase, "Verb" if it is a verb phrase.

1. A girl <u>is jumping</u> <u>on the trampoline</u>.   (2)
         Verb   **Prep**

2. At the movies the usher was giving toys to the children.   (3)

3. After school some students will be playing with their friends.   (3)

4. The coach is talking to his players inside the dugout.   (3)

5. Alicia has been reading a letter from her mom for an hour.   (3)

6. A ball has rolled against the fence.   (2)

7. Yolanda must be working really hard on her test.   (2)

8. In a month we will be taking a test on the body systems.   (3)

Extension: Write each preposition below in a phrase.

after	behind	for	of	over
up	against	below	from	on

Phrases
#4

I. Directions: If the phrase below is a prepositional phrase, write "Prep" on the line. If the phrase is a verb phrase, write "Verb."

_____ 1. from Dad

_____ 2. will be working

_____ 3. has been singing

_____ 4. beside the teacher

_____ 5. does help

_____ 6. without any money

_____ 7. has thought

_____ 8. during recess

_____ 9. can read

_____ 10. inside the box

II. Underline all the phrases in each sentence. Below the phrase, write "Prep" if it is a prepositional phrase, "Verb" if it is a verb phrase.

1. Some penguins <u>were diving</u> <u>into the water</u>. (2)
                     Verb   **Prep**

2. A funny looking bird with spiky hair was squawking at the children. (3)

3. At the mall a man in a clown suit was making animal balloons. (3)

4. The children had played for five minutes at recess. (3)

5. Mom does clean in my room every day. (2)

6. Everyone in our class will be making a card for Valentine's Day. (3)

7. The girl in the pink sweater is riding my bike. (2)

8. Alma must be studying for her test at the library. (3)

Extension: Write each verb phrase below in a sentence.

had played   **is riding**   **will be making**   **does clean**

Phrases
#5

Directions: Use any subject, prepositional phrase, and verb phrase from
below to write sentences.

Subject	Verb Phrase	Prepositional Phrase
The dog	can run	across the sky
A cow	is walking	in the mud
Birds	will work	~~outside the fence~~
Mice	was chewing	around the barn
A plane	had slept	on a bone
Several ants	~~had escaped~~	outside my window
The farmer	were chirping	through a maze
The pigs	was flying	into the kitchen
~~Some chickens~~	might crawl	in the field

1. ___ **Some chickens had escaped outside the fence.**_____

2. _____

3. _____

4. _____

5. _____

6. _____

7. _____

8. _____

9. _____

Fragment and Run-on Sentences
#1

A **sentence** tells a <u>complete thought</u>.

A **fragment** sentence does not tell a complete thought. It might be missing the subject (who? or what?) or the predicate (what the subject is or does).

A fragment missing the <u>subject</u> - Riding on his bike.

A fragment missing the <u>predicate</u> - The best game in the world.

Directions: If the sentence below is a fragment, write "fragment." If it is a complete thought, write "sentence."

_____ 1. Swinging back and forth on the swing.

_____ 2. We went down the slide head first.

_____ 3. The boys played basketball.

_____ 4. Crawling in the grass.

_____ 5. Ants all over our picnic table.

_____ 6. Dora had an adventure.

_____ 7. The ghost in the attic.

_____ 8. Dolphins live in the ocean.

_____ 9. The puppy will bark for a treat.

_____ 10. Making cookies with my sister.

Extension: There are five (5) fragment sentences on this worksheet. Rewrite the fragment sentences by adding words to complete the thought.

Fragment and Run-on Sentences
#2

> A **sentence** tells a <u>complete thought</u>.
> A **run-on** sentence has two or more complete thoughts.
> **Run-on:** Kristy collects stuffed animals she keeps them on her bed.
> **Two Complete Thoughts:** Kristy collects stuffed animals.
> She keeps them on her bed.

Directions: Rewrite each run-on sentence below. Turn them into two complete sentences. You may need to add some words.

1. Mom made a dress for my party it was beautiful.

   _____

2. We went to the park then our teacher planted some flowers.

   _____

3. Toucans are beautiful birds they live in the jungle.

   _____

4. Crystal went on the swing she went very high.

   _____

5. Bobby made a sandcastle then he went into the water.

   _____

6. Our parrot is funny he can tell a knock-knock joke.

   _____

7. I played in the mud my Mom is going to be mad.

   _____

8. A button fell off of my shirt it landed in my soup.

   _____

Fragment and Run-on Sentences
#3

Directions: For each sentence below write F if the sentence is a fragment,
RO if it is a run-on, and S if it is a complete sentence.

_____ 1. The phone rang.

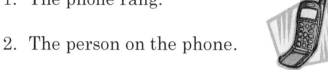

_____ 2. The person on the phone.

_____ 3. We talked for hours it was nice.

_____ 4. Played in the sand.

_____ 5. A wave came it knocked over our castle.

_____ 6. My brother laughed at our wet castle.

_____ 7. The girls ran to the playground they played tetherball.

_____ 8. Gloria was the first to win a game.

_____ 9. Swinging as hard as she could.

_____ 10. The lion is the king of the jungle.

_____ 11. A lion with big ferocious teeth.

_____ 12. The lion roared all the animals ran.

Extension: There are four (4) fragment sentences on this worksheet.
Rewrite the fragment sentences by adding words to complete the
thought.

Fragment and Run-on Sentences
#4

Directions: For each sentence below write F if the sentence is a fragment, RO if it is a run-on, and S if it is a complete sentence.

_____ 1. The best carnival in the world.

_____ 2. John won a prize at the carnival.

_____ 3. He threw the ball the milk bottles crashed.

_____ 4. Our family went to the game.

_____ 5. Cheering for our favorite team.

_____ 6. A horn blew we all yelled.

_____ 7. Coach let me be goalie I stopped three shots.

_____ 8. Diving across the grass to stop the ball.

_____ 9. Jose is a great soccer player.

_____ 10. Sledding head first down the hill.

_____ 11. It snowed all night then we played all day.

_____ 12. We raced down the hill on our sleds.

Extension: Fix all of the run-on sentences from this worksheet.

Fragment and Run-on Sentences
#5

Directions: The story below is one giant run-on sentence.
1. Circle every "and" and "then".
2. Rewrite the story. Replace every "and" and "then" with a period. Capitalize the next word.

I had the best birthday party ever and all of my friends were there and we hit a piñata then we played games in our back yard then we ate ice cream with any topping we wanted and then I got to open my presents and it was the greatest party ever.

Rewrite the story:

_____

_____

_____

_____

_____

_____

_____

_____

Titles or
Topic Sentences #1

Topic Sentence:

In a paragraph, the topic sentence tells the main idea of the paragraph. Many young writers confuse a title with a topic sentence. What is wrong with the topic sentence below?

The most exciting day of my life.

This would make a good title, but it is a fragment sentence. The box below explains how to make a title. Use these rules to write good titles. However, make sure your topic sentences make a complete thought.

Titles
1. Capitalize the first, last, and all the important words.
2. Do not capitalize A, An, The, and prepositions that are less than 5 letters unless they are the first or last word of the title.
3. Capitalize prepositions that are 5 words or more.

Examples: **The Longest Day** of the **Year** / **Hope Without Fear**

Directions: Are the statements below titles or topic sentences? Write "sentence" if the statement is a sentence. If it is a title, rewrite it by using the rules of capitalization.

1. The longest day of the year. _____The Longest Day of the Year_____

2. Spot is a funny dog. _____

3. Hope without fear. _____

4. My favorite toy. _____

5. The biggest tree house in the world. _____

6. You'll never believe what I did yesterday. _____

7. Singing a song in the chorus. _____

8. America is the best country in the world. _____

Titles or
Topic Sentences #2

Name: _____

Directions: For each statement below, write "title" if it is a title. Write "sentence" if it is a sentence.

_____ 1. The longest day of the year.

_____ 2. It was the longest day of the year.

_____ 3. We took the long way home.

_____ 4. The long way home.

_____ 5. Three wishes for everyone.

_____ 6. The genie gave three wishes.

_____ 7. I wrote a letter for my teacher.

_____ 8. A letter for my teacher.

_____ 9. Sean had a surprise party.

_____ 10. A surprise party for Sean.

_____ 11. The Fourth of July picnic.

_____ 12. Our family had a picnic on the Fourth of July.

_____ 13. Attack of the hungry squirrels.

_____ 14. The camp was attacked by hungry squirrels.

_____ 15. Great topic sentences.

Extension: You know that titles need to have all the important words capitalized. In the worksheet above, there are eight (8) titles. Rewrite all the titles from above so that all the important words are capitalized.

Remember to capitalize the first, last, and all the important words. A, An, The, and all prepositions that are five letters or less should not be capitalized unless they are the first or last words.

Example: The black cat.   The **Black Cat**

CreateBetterWriters.com   152

Name: _____

Titles or
Topic Sentences #3

Directions: For each statement below, write "title" if it is a title. Write "sentence" if it is a sentence.

_____ 1. The best pizza in the world.

_____ 2. My mouth had a party.

_____ 3. The day of the big race.

_____ 4. It was the day of the big race.

_____ 5. Tammy and I are best friends.

_____ 6. Best friends forever.

_____ 7. Wrestling in the dirt.

_____ 8. The boys were wrestling in the dirt.

_____ 9. I taught Fido silly dog tricks.

_____ 10. Silly dog tricks.

_____ 11. It rained like crazy today.

_____ 12. Rain from the sky.

_____ 13. My dad played a funny joke on me.

_____ 14. Funny joke by my dad.

_____ 15. Complete thoughts for topic sentences.

Extension: Rewrite all eight (8) of the titles from above. Follow the rules for capitalizing titles. Use the space below the titles.

CreateBetterWriters.com   153

Subject-Verb Agreement
#1

What is wrong with the sentences below?

#1 Andre ride his skateboard very well.

#2 Brian and Tom is my best friends.

These sentences break the **subject-verb agreement** rule. If the subject of the sentence is singular (one thing), the verb must be singular. If the subject in the sentence is plural (more than one thing), the verb must be plural.

What is the subject of sentence #1? Andre   (Singular)

What is the verb of sentence #1? ride (Plural)

Singular verbs need an "s" or "es".   Andre <u>rides</u> his skateboard very well.

Plural verbs do not have an "s".   They <u>ride</u> their skateboards very well.

Other singular verbs: "is" and "was"
Other plural verbs: "are" and "were"

Brian and Tom <u>are</u> my best friends.
Tom <u>is</u> my best friend.

Directions: Are the subjects below singular or plural? 1. Underline the subject in each sentence. 2. Below the subjects write S if it is singular or P if it is plural. 3. Circle the verb that fits the sentence.

1. <u>Omar</u> (buy , (buys)) a new video game every year.
   S

2. Several large, hairy spiders (make , makes) webs in our yard.

3. The girls on the bench (is , are) doing their homework.

4. The water in the buckets (is , are) very dirty so don't drink it.

5. Many hungry customers (order , orders) large meals.

6. My dad (watch , watches) football every Sunday.

7. The boys on the bed (play , plays) rough.

8. Our team (was , were) ready to play.

Subject-Verb Agreement
#2

Name: _____

I. Are the subjects below singular or plural? 1. Underline the subject in each sentence. 2. Below the subjects write S if it is singular or P if it is plural. 3. Circle the verb that fits the sentence.

1. The children (eat , eats) very quickly.

2. Our teacher (is , are) getting ready for our test.

3. Babies in the nursery (climb , climbs) all over the toys.

4. Every December Chris (write , writes) a letter to Santa.

5. Thomas, using his colored pencils, (draw , draws) amazing pictures.

6. We (is , are) going to the library today.

7. The people in the village always (wash , washes) in the river.

8. When students finish their drawings, they (color , colors) the pictures.

9. The dress with the pretty flowers (was , were) beautiful.

10. Players in the game (throw , throws) beanbags on the squares.

II. Write C on the line if each sentence below has a correct subject and verb. Write I if it is incorrect. If incorrect, then change the verb to make it correct.

__I__ 1. Amy ~~read~~ every night before she goes to bed.
         reads

_____ 2. The cowboys rides their horses.

_____ 3. At the rodeo a clown chase the bull to protect the bull riders.

_____ 4. The dancers in the parade wear beautiful costumes.

_____ 5. Whenever we have pizza my dog bark until he gets a bite.

_____ 6. The man with the guitar plays very well.

CreateBetterWriters.com   155

Subject-Verb Agreement
#3

I. Are the subjects below singular or plural? 1. Underline the subject in each sentence. 2. Below the subjects write S if it is singular or P if it is plural. 3. Circle the verb that fits the sentence.

1. The jet (fly , flys) quickly across the sky.

2. Doctors at the hospital (was , were) ready to help.

3. Every day the coaches (teach , teaches) us a new skill.

4. If the boys with the telescope (look, looks) closely, they can see the planet.

5. Many people (think , thinks) that writing is fun.

6. The reporters said that our school (is , are) the best.

7. The president of the soccer leagues (feel , feels) we are doing well.

8. When she (touch , touches) the turtle's head, it hides in its shell.

II. Write C on the line if each sentence below has a correct subject and verb. Write I if it is incorrect. If incorrect, then change the verb to make it correct.

_____ 1. Many cars races around the track very quickly.

_____ 2. Mrs. Smith always shows us better ways to study.

_____ 3. During the slumber party the girls hits each other with pillows.

_____ 4. Dad tell ghost stories and scare us a lot.

_____ 5. My brothers play with their remote control cars all the time.

_____ 6. Our choir sing five songs at every show.

Extension: Write each verb below in a sentence. Underline your subject in each sentence. Write "singular" or "plural" below it.

plays   **read**   **are**   **cuts**   **talk**

Example: <u>Mary</u> **plays** with her dolls.
Singular

Subject-Verb Agreement
#4

Name: _____

I. **Directions**: Write a verb on the line in each sentence that fits the subject-verb rule. Keep all of the verbs in the <u>present</u> tense.

1. Every day a man _____ past our house.

2. We all _____ our new folders.

3. Every time my dad jogs he _____ a lot of water.

4. Babies don't know how to talk so they _____ to get what they want.

5. Jenny _____ her stuffed animals when she is happy.

6. If you _____ a good story, you will get a good grade.

7. The children _____ a lot during recess.

8. He always _____ when it rains.

II. Below is a story. As you read it you will notice that the subject-verb agreement rule has been broken many times. Each time the rule is broken, cross out the verb and rewrite it in the space below.

Every day when I ~~walks~~ home from school, a big black dog chase me down my
walk
block. It see me coming when I turn the corner. My sister run the other way, but I

choose to face it. I stands firm with my fists high in the air and I yells, "Aaaahhhh."

Dogs hates when you do that. They thinks you are big and powerful so they runs

away. My sister are too afraid to try it. I don't blames her. Sometimes when I tries

it, some dogs knocks me over. I guess it would be safer for us if we takes another way

home. It are not good to mess with strange dogs.

Did you find all 14?

Chapter 6
Review

I. Phrases

Directions: Underline all the phrases in each sentence. Below the phrase, write "Prep" if it is a prepositional phrase or "Verb" if it is a verb phrase.

1. A girl <u>is jumping</u> <u>on the trampoline</u>.   (2)
           Verb   Prep

2. Before the game the coach was talking to the players.   (3)

3. After lunch some students were playing in the sandbox.   (3)

4. Mom is making cookies in the kitchen.   (2)

5. Amy will be walking to school.   (2)

6. The puppy in the corner is sleeping on its new bed.   (3)

II. Fragment and Run-On Sentences

Directions: For each sentence below write F if the sentence is a fragment, RO if it is a run-on, and S if it is a complete sentence.

_____ 1. The dog barked.

_____ 2. The dog in the yard.

_____ 3. We pet the puppy it was nice.

_____ 4. Making cookies in the kitchen.

_____ 5. Mom poured the mix I stirred it.

_____ 6. The cookies tasted great.

_____ 7. I read a good book.

_____ 8. The book was funny I read it again.

_____ 9. The best book I ever read.

III. Title or Topic Sentence

Directions: For each statement below, write "title" if it is a title. Write "sentence" if it is a sentence.

_____ 1. The happiest day of my life.

_____ 2. It was the happiest day of my life.

_____ 3. I was drawing a picture for Mom.

_____ 4. Drawing a picture for Mom.

_____ 5. Free ice cream for everyone.

IV. Subject-Verb Agreement

Directions: Write C on the line if each sentence below has a correct subject and verb. Write I if it is incorrect. If incorrect, then change the verb to make it correct.

_____ 1. My dad drive to work every day.

_____ 2. The bunnies hop all around the yard.

_____ 3. The singers is ready to go.

_____ 4. The girls in the car fix their hair.

_____ 5. While the band plays, the players practices their drills.

Chapter 6
Test

I. Phrases

Directions: Underline all the phrases in each sentence. Below the phrase, write "Prep" if it is a prepositional phrase, "Verb" if it is a verb phrase.

1. A cat is climbing up a tree.   (2)

2. The doctor was looking into my ears.   (2)

3. In the morning they were making breakfast in the kitchen.   (3)

4. Zoo keepers will be feeding the bears at noon.   (2)

5. The lady with the funny hat was reading under the tree.   (3)

II. Fragment and Run-On Sentences

Directions: For each sentence below write " if the sentence is a fragment RO if it is a run-on, and S if it is a complete sentence.

_____ 1. Honking the horn.

_____ 2. The driver honked the horn.

_____ 3. He honked the horn then we all looked.

_____ 4. The swings were fun we went high.

_____ 5. A day at the park.

_____ 6. It was a fun day at the park.

_____ 7. My birthday is my favorite day of the year.

_____ 8. It was my birthday I had a party.

_____ 9. My favorite day of the year.

III. Title or Topic Sentence

Directions: For each statement below, write "title" if it is a title. Write "sentence" if it is a sentence.

_____ 1. Superman is the strongest man in the world.

_____ 2. The strongest man in the world.

_____ 3. A big, juicy hamburger with cheese.

_____ 4. He made a big, juicy hamburger with cheese.

_____ 5. The store gave free ice cream to everyone.

IV. Subject-Verb Agreement

Directions: Write C on the line if each sentence below has a correct subject and verb. Write I if it is incorrect. If incorrect, then change the verb to make it correct.

_____ 1. Tina work very hard.

_____ 2. Frogs eat a lot of flies.

_____ 3. My friend are going with me.

_____ 4. The captain of the team play the best.

_____ 5. When the teacher takes roll, the students turn in homework.

Chapter 6
Test - Answer Key

I. Phrases

Directions: Underline all the phrases in each sentence. Below the phrase, write "Prep" if it is a prepositional phrase, "Verb" if it is a verb phrase.

1. A cat <u>is climbing</u> <u>up a tree</u>.   (2)
          Verb   **Prep**

2. The doctor <u>was looking</u> <u>into my ears</u>.   (2)
          Verb   **Prep**

3. <u>In the morning</u> they <u>were making</u> breakfast <u>in the kitchen</u>.   (3)
  Prep   **Verb**   **Prep**

4. Zoo keepers <u>will be feeding</u> the bears <u>at noon</u>.   (2)
          Verb   **Prep**

5. The lady <u>with the funny hat</u> <u>was reading</u> <u>under the tree</u>.   (3)
     Prep   **Verb**   **Prep**

II. Fragment and Run-On Sentences

Directions: For each sentence below write "F" if the sentence is a fragment, "RO" if it is a run-on, and "S" if it is a complete sentence.

F 1. Honking the horn.

S 2. The driver honked the horn.

RO 3. He honked the horn then we all looked.

RO 4. The swings were fun we went high.

F 5. A day at the park.

S 6. It was a fun day at the park.

S 7. My birthday is my favorite day of the year.

RO 8. It was my birthday I had a party.

F 9. My favorite day of the year.

III. Title or Topic Sentence

Directions: For each statement below, write "title" if it is a title. Write "sentence" if it is a sentence.

Sentence   1. Superman is the strongest man in the world.

Title   2. The strongest man in the world.

Title   3. A big, juicy hamburger with cheese.

Sentence   4. He made a big, juicy hamburger with cheese.

Sentence   5. The store gave free ice cream to everyone.

IV. Subject-Verb Agreement

Directions: Write "C" on the line if each sentence below has a correct subject and verb. Write "I" if it is incorrect. If incorrect, then change the verb to make it correct.

I   1. Tina ~~work~~ very hard.
       works

C   2. Frogs eat a lot of flies.

I   3. My friend ~~are~~ going with me.
       is

I   4. The captain of the team ~~play~~ the best.
       plays

C   5. When the teacher takes roll, the students turn in homework.

Unit 7

Homonyms

Compound Words

A vs. An

Grammar Standards – Unit 7

_____
Student

	Mastery	Non-Mastery
1. Homonyms		
2. Compound Words		
3. A vs. An		

Grammar Standards – Unit 7

_____
Student

	Mastery	Non-Mastery
1. Homonyms		
2. Compound Words		
3. A vs. An		

Homonyms
Group #1

Homonyms (homophones) are words that sound the same but are different in spelling or meaning.

In the box below are five (5) groups of homonyms. Use these worksheets to learn the differences between the words.

Homonyms
Group #1

there – tells about a place   Example: Put the book <u>there</u>.
their – belonging to someone   Example: This is <u>their</u> room.
they're – contraction for "they are" Example: <u>They're</u> nice.

no – a negative response   Example: <u>No</u>, you cant' go.
know – to understand something Example: I <u>know</u> how to swim.

to – connecting word.   Example: We went <u>to</u> school.
two – the number 2   Example: We have <u>two</u> eyes.
too – also or extreme amount   Example: He's <u>too</u> young <u>too</u>.

won – past tense of win   Example: They <u>won</u> the game.
one – the number 1   Example: I have <u>one</u> nose.

son – parents male child   Example: He looks like his <u>son</u>.
sun – the star in the center   Example: The <u>sun</u> is bright.
    of our solar system

Study the Homonyms

Make study pictures for each homonym. A study picture is a way of tricking yourself into remembering the differences between the two (or three) words.

Example: Sun has a "u" / Son has an "o". Draw a sun in the shape of a "U".

Sun	Son

Homonyms

```
Homonyms - Group #1
there, their, they're    no, know    to, two, too,
    won, one,        sun, son
```

I. On a separate sheet of paper, write each homonym from Group #1 in a sentence.

II. Read your sentences to a partner. Ask them to spell the homonym from each of your sentences.

III. Fill in the blanks with a word from Homonym Group #1.

1. _____ going to be late tonight.

2. He threw the ball _____ me.

3. The dad and his _____ will be on the same team.

4. Mom said _____ but Dad said yes.

5. We went to _____ house to do our homework.

6. The Angels played hard and _____ the game.

7. Everyone has _____ eyes and one mouth.

8. Put the box over _____.

9. After the rain the _____ finally came out.

10. The field was _____ wet for us to play today.

11. If you multiply any number by _____ the answer will be itself.

12. We all _____ how to multiply by five.

Homonyms
Group #1 - Practice

Homonyms - Group #1
there, their, they're   no, know   to, two, too,
won, one,   sun, son

Directions: Fill in the blanks with a word from Homonym Group #1.

1. We _____ someone who can fix your bike.

2. Jennifer kicked a goal, and we _____ the game.

3. The light from the _____ is bright today.

4. It was _____ windy to go on the rides.

5. _____ is a big spider on the sink.

6. There was only _____ donut left so I let him have it.

7. The class put _____ backpacks against the wall.

8. After dinner I wasn't hungry so I said _____ to dessert.

9. I always have two pencils in case _____ breaks.

10. They walked all the way _____ the store.

11. _____ the best players on the team.

12. John is his dad's oldest _____.

Extension: Write the following homonyms in a sentence:
there   **their**   **know**   **too**   **son**

Homonyms
Group #2

Homonyms (homophones) are words that sound the same but are different in spelling or meaning.

In the box below are five (5) groups of homonyms. Use these worksheets to learn the differences between the words.

Homonyms
Group #2

steal – taking what is not yours   Example: Don't <u>steal</u>.
steel – strong iron alloy   Example: It's as strong as <u>steal</u>.

ate – past tense of eat   Example: She <u>ate</u> the pizza.
eight – the number 8   Example: A squid has <u>eight</u> arms.

blue – the color blue / sad   Example: She felt <u>blue</u> yesterday.
blew – past tense of blow   Example: The wind <u>blew</u> all day.

here – this place   Example: Put the book <u>here</u>.
hear – able to take in sound   Example: Can you <u>hear</u> me?

close – to shut   Example: Don't <u>close</u> the door.
clothes – garments that cover the body   Example: Wash your <u>clothes</u>.

Study the Homonyms

Make study pictures for each homonym. A study picture is a way of tricking yourself into remembering the differences between the two (or three) words.

Example: Blue is a color and means sad.   Blew has a "w" just like "wind".

Blue	**Blew**
	Blew
	i
	n
She is blue and cries blue tears.	d

Name: _____

Homonyms

Homonyms - Group #2

steal, steel   ate, eight   blue, blew
here, hear   close, clothes

I. On a separate sheet of paper, write each homonym from Group #2 in a sentence.

II. Read your sentences to a partner. Ask them to spell the homonym from each of your sentences.

III. Fill in the blanks with a word from Homonym Group #2.

    1. The wind _____ hard for over an hour.

    2. If you _____ you might go to jail.

    3. An octopus has _____ legs called tentacles.

    4. We all received new _____ for our birthdays.

    5. The noise made it hard for us to _____ the television.

    6. Don't forget to _____ the door.

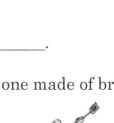

    7. Who _____ all of the pizza?

    8. I love when there are no clouds and the sky is _____.

    9. The building made of _____ is stronger than the one made of bricks.

    10. The teacher told us to wait _____.

    11. Rover _____ all of our hotdogs.

    12. She fell into a puddle and got her _____ all wet.

Homonyms
Group #2 - Practice

Name: _____

Homonyms - Group #2
steal, steel   ate, eight   blue, blew
here, hear   close, clothes

Directions: Fill in the blanks with a word from Homonym Group #2.

1. I can't believe that my dog _____ my shoe.

2. Turn up the television so we can _____ better.

3. It was cold because Tim didn't _____ the door.

4. _____ paint and yellow paint will make green paint.

5. My dog buried my shoe right _____.

6. Our teacher always wears nice _____.

7. Dad _____ out the candles on his cake.

8. Maria swam _____ laps in the pool.

9. If you listen carefully you will _____ the ocean.

10. Bank robbers tried to _____ the money.

11. The wind _____ all night and knocked over the trees.

12. The bank robbers were locked behind _____ bars.

Extension: Write the following homonyms in a sentence:
steal   clothes   close   hear   here

Homonyms
Group #3

Homonyms (homophones) are words that sound the same but are different in spelling or meaning.

In the box below are five (5) groups of homonyms. Use these worksheets to learn the differences between the words.

Homonyms
Group #3

weigh – to measure something's weight	Example: How much do you <u>weigh</u>?
way – direction / how to do something	Example: Go this way. Do it the right <u>way</u>.
week – seven days	Example: We'll be here for a <u>week</u>.
weak – not much strength	Example: The heat made us <u>weak</u>.
I'll – contraction for "I will"	Example: <u>I'll</u> be ready.
aisle – path between seats	Example: Walk down the <u>aisle</u>.
isle – small island	Example: The <u>isle</u> was beautiful.
threw – past tense of throw	Example: He <u>threw</u> the ball.
through – traveling across the middle of	Example: The plane went <u>through</u> the clouds.
flew – past tense of fly	Example: The bird <u>flew</u> away.
flu – sickness, short for influenza	Example: She had the <u>flu</u>.

Study the Homonyms

Make study pictures for each homonym. A study picture is a way of tricking yourself into remembering the differences between the two (or three) words.

Example: Flew and wind have a "W"

You "U" have the flu.

Flew
Flew
i
n
d
The birds flew through the wind.

Flu

Homonyms

Homonyms - Group #3
weigh, way   week, weak   I'll, aisle, isle
threw, through   flew, flu

I. On a separate sheet of paper, write each homonym from Group #3 in a sentence.

II. Read your sentences to a partner. Ask them to spell the homonym in each sentence.

III. Fill in the blanks with a word from Homonym Group #1.

1. In one _____ it will be summer vacation.

2. A bird _____ into the house.

3. The usher walked down the _____ with us.

4. The doctor will _____ you on his scale at his office.

5. The boat crashed on an _____ in the middle of the ocean.

6. Jimmy _____ the ball over the fence.

7. He was sick so he was too _____ to go to school.

8. Too many people are sick with the _____.

9. Do you know the _____ to Grandmother's house?

10. _____ study hard for my test.

11. A car crashed _____ a wall.

12. On the bus, would you like a window seat or an _____ seat?

Homonyms
Group #3 - Practice

Homonyms - Group #3
weigh, way   week, weak   I'll, aisle, isle
threw, through   flew, flu

Directions: Fill in the blanks with a word from Homonym Group #3.

1. The store will _____ the candy which costs $2.25 a pound.

2. We had to walk home _____ the rain.

3. The chair broke because it was too _____.

4. _____ ask if you can sleep over tonight.

5. We all got a _____ shot so we wouldn't get sick.

6. The ship sailed out to a small _____ in the ocean.

7. He _____ his trash into the garbage.

8. Lee _____ his kite very high at the park.

9. The bride walked down the center _____ at the wedding.

10. She does everything the right _____.

11. Our family spent a _____ at the lake.

12. I ate healthy so I _____ less than I did last month.

Extension: Write the following homonyms in a sentence:
weigh   **weak**   **aisle**   **threw**   **flu**

Homonyms
Review
#1

Name: _____

Group #1:	there, their, they're, no, know, to, two, too, won, one, sun, son
Group #2:	steal, steel, ate, eight, blue, blew, here, hear, close, clothes
Group #3:	weight, way, week, weak, I'll, aisle, isle, threw, through, flew, flu

Directions: Fill in the blanks with a word from Homonym Groups #1, #2, or #3.

1. Do you want one sandwich or _____?

2. The American flag is red, white, and _____.

3. Do you _____ how to ride a bike?

4. _____ is much stronger than wood.

5. Yesterday he put his book on the table, but today it wasn't _____.

6. _____ the window so flies can't come in.

7. Bob and his _____ work together at the store.

8. My muscles are too _____ to lift these weights.

9. Mom went _____ the store.

10. When I ask my dad if I can play with his glasses he says _____.

11. Cameras are ready to catch anyone who might _____ something.

12. The wolf huffed and puffed and _____ his house down.

13. _____ not ready to start the game.

14. On Sunday we put on our best _____ for the party.

15. Spring break only lasts for a _____.

16. The boat stopped at a small _____ in the ocean.

CreateBetterWriters.com   176

Homonyms Review #2

Group #1:	there, their, they're, no, know, to, two, too, won, one, sun, son
Group #2:	steal, steel, ate, eight, blue, blew, here, hear, close, clothes
Group #3:	weigh, way, week, weak, I'll, aisle, isle, threw, through, flew, flu

Directions: Fill in the blanks with a word from Homonym Groups #1, #2, or #3.

1. When we got home it was _____ late to watch television.

2. We _____ a lot of pizza at the party.

3. Did you _____ that loud explosion?

4. They covered _____ books to keep them protected.

5. The bus driver can't find his _____ to the camp.

6. Our team was excited because we _____ the game.

7. _____ be ready in two minutes.

8. The quarterback _____ a pass to the receiver.

9. An octagon has _____ sides.

10. Wait _____, and I'll be back in a minute.

11. Step on the scale to see how much you _____.

12. Only _____ person at a time can play.

13. He put on dark glasses because the _____ was so bright.

14. The children ran _____ the puddle.

15. My seats are right on the _____ near the usher.

16. The plane _____ right over our heads.

Compound Words
#1

Name: _____

Compound means "made from two or more things".

A **compound word** is a word made by putting two words together.

Examples: hot + dog = hotdog   dog + house = doghouse

I. Combine the words below to form compound words.

1. every + body

_____

2. hand + shake

_____

3. card + board

_____

4. snow + ball

_____

5. rain + drop

_____

6. mail + box

_____

7. pop + corn

_____

8. blue + berry

_____

9. sail + boat

_____

10. eye + sight

_____

II. Make compound words by taking a word from Box A and putting it with Box B.

Box A		
~~news~~	chalk	air
waste	water	sea
thunder	snow	quick

Box B		
board	plane	storm
basket	proof	flake
sand	shore	~~paper~~

1. __**newspaper**___   4. _____   7. _____

2. _____   5. _____   8. _____

3. _____   6. _____   9. _____

Compound Words
#2

I. Combine the words below to form compound words.

1. side + walk

   _____

2. meat + ball

   _____

3. drive + way

   _____

4. trash + can

   _____

5. flash + light

   _____

6. key + chain

   _____

II. Underline the compound word in each sentence. Write the two words that form the compound word on the lines.

1. She has posters all over her bedroom walls. _____ _____

2. Amy drew hearts all over her notebook. _____ _____

3. The sidewalk has several cracks. _____ _____

4. The car went up the driveway. _____ _____

5. My birthday is in two weeks. _____ _____

6. He's the best shortstop on the team. _____ _____

7. John threw a baseball through a window. _____ _____

8. The toy was on top of the bookshelf. _____ _____

9. Spaghetti tastes good with a meatball. _____ _____

10. Dad gets a paycheck every two weeks. _____ _____

Extension: Select any five (5) compound words from this page. Write each one in a sentence.

Compound Words
#3

boy	space	tooth	finger
friend	ship	brush	nail
skate	land	under	race
board	slide	ground	horse
sea	water	class	melon
gull	fall	color	paper
super	eye	every	sand
market	sight	body	castle
life	earth	home	room
guard	quake	work	bed

I. Use the words in the box to form compound words. Write at least twenty compound words on the lines below. You may use a word from the box more than once.

_____

_____

_____

_____

_____

_____

II. Underline the compound word in each sentence. Write the two words that form the compound word on the lines.

1. We went to police headquarters. _____ _____

2. The trashcan was full of garbage. _____ _____

3. Mom eats oatmeal every morning. _____ _____

4. The flashlight needs new batteries. _____ _____

5. I need a keychain for my keys. _____ _____

A vs. An
#1

> **A vs. An**
> Use "a" when the next word starts with a consonant.
> Examples: **a** <u>b</u>all , **a** <u>h</u>at, **a** <u>d</u>og, **a** <u>f</u>ish, **a** <u>z</u>ebra
>
> Use "an" when the next word starts with a vowel or vowel sound.
> Examples: **an** <u>a</u>pple , **an** <u>e</u>agle, **an** <u>i</u>ceberg,
> **an** <u>o</u>live, **an** <u>u</u>mbrella **an** <u>h</u>onor

I. Write five (5) words that would follow "a". Next, write five (5) words that would follow "an".

A   **An**
Example: a cat   Example: an egg

_____   _____

_____   _____

_____   _____

_____   _____

_____   _____

II. Fill in each blank with "a" or "an".

1. We saw _____ eagle flying past _____ nest.

2. Is _____ aardvark also called _____ anteater?

3. The teacher asked _____ question, but I didn't have _____ answer.

4. _____ car had _____ accident about _____ hour ago.

5. Tom wants to be _____ actor or _____ lawyer.

6. _____ guide will lead us on _____ adventure through the woods.

7. Will _____ airbag protect _____ passenger in _____ crash?

8. _____ crocodile looks a lot like _____ alligator.

A vs. An
#2

Name: _____

I. Fill in each blank with "a" or "an".

1. There was ____ Canadian, ____ American, and ____ Asian on the plane.

2. _____ aluminum can should be recycled.

3. Jennifer was _____ actress who played _____ angel in the play.

4. If there is ____ ant on ____ picnic blanket, there will soon be more ants.

5. At the zoo we saw _____ zebra, _____ monkey, and _____ elephant.

6. _____ apple would be _____ good snack at recess.

7. Do you live in _____ house or _____ apartment?

8. _____ manager asked him to fill out _____ application.

9. We have _____ orange tree, but I really want _____ avocado tree.

10. _____ Eskimo might catch _____ fish and live in _____ igloo.

II. You are on a nature hike. Write a story about things you see and do. Use "an" and "a" at least five times.

_____

_____

_____

_____

_____

_____

_____

_____

A vs. An
#3

Name: _____

I. Fill in each blank with "a" or "an".

1. _____ ice cream truck came by so I bought _____ popsicle.

2. We need _____ umbrella or _____ hood for our jackets.

3. It will take _____ army of people to make _____ new bridge.

4. _____ artist drew _____ picture of _____ sunset.

5. _____ office at our school has _____ letter for you.

6. For breakfast I had _____ pancake, _____ sausage, and _____ egg.

7. I think _____ armadillo has a shell to protect it from _____ predator.

8. They need _____ umpire for _____ baseball game.

9. _____ student wrote _____ article about _____ field trip.

10. _____ tree fell so we chopped it up with _____ ax.

II. You are grocery shopping with your mom. Write about the things you see, do, and buy in the store. Use "an" and "a" at least five times.

_____

_____

_____

_____

_____

_____

_____

_____

_____

Chapter 7
Test

I. Homonyms:

> **Group #1:** there, their, they're, no, know, to, two, too, won, one, sun, son
> **Group #2:** steal, steel, ate, eight, blue, blew, here, hear, close, clothes
> **Group #3:** weigh, way, week, weak, I'll, aisle, isle, threw, through, flew, flu

Directions: Fill in the blanks with a word from Homonym Groups #1, #2, or #3.

1. The teacher told them to turn in _____ homework.

2. The fan _____ cool air on us.

3. Our team _____ the game.

4. Because she was sick, she was too _____ to go outside.

5. I stood on the scale to see how much I _____.

6. The bird _____ onto my finger.

7. She put on nice _____ for the party.

8. The usher stood in the middle of the _____.

9. Do you _____ your ABC's or did you forget them?

10. Are you seven or _____ years old?

11. Don't _____ cookies from the jar, or you'll get in trouble.

12. She _____ her trash away.

13. The truck driver was _____ tired to keep driving.

14. Can you _____ the music from next door.

15. John has two daughters and one _____ named John Jr.

II. Compound Words

Directions: Underline the compound word in each sentence. Write the two words that form the compound word on the lines.

1. He cleaned his teeth with a toothpick. _____ _____

2. A newspaper has useful information. _____ _____

3. He tripped on the crack in the sidewalk. _____ _____

4. She gave a haircut to my mother. _____ _____

5. The police found a fingerprint on the door. _____ _____

III. A vs. An

Directions: Fill in each blank with "a" or "an".

1. _____ man in the park made _____ elephant out of a balloon.

2. Karen wanted _____ apple for _____ snack.

3. Mrs. Smith is _____ new teacher with _____ easy class.

4. During the storm we need boots, _____ rain coat, and _____ umbrella.

5. There was _____ emergency phone call from _____ doctor.

Chapter 7
Test - Answer Key

I. Homonyms:

Group #1: there, their, they're, no, know, to, two, too, won, one, sun, son
Group #2: steal, steel, ate, eight, blue, blew, here, hear, close, clothes
Group #3: weigh, way, week, weak, I'll, aisle, isle, threw, through, flew, flu

Directions: Fill in the blanks with a word from Homonym Groups #1, #2, or #3.

1. The teacher told them to turn in __their__ homework.

2. The fan __blew__ cool air on us.

3. Our team __won__ the game.

4. Because she was sick, she was too __weak__ to go outside.

5. I stood on the scale to see how much I __weigh__.

6. The bird __flew__ onto my finger.

7. She put on nice __clothes__ for the party.

8. The usher stood in the middle of the __aisle__.

9. Do you __know__ your ABC's or did you forget them?

10. Are you seven or __eight__ years old?

11. Don't __steal__ cookies from the jar, or you'll get in trouble.

12. She __threw__ her trash away.

13. The truck driver was __too__ tired to keep driving.

14. Can you __hear__ the music from next door.

15. John has two daughters and one __son__ named John Jr.

II. Compound Words

Directions: Underline the compound word in each sentence. Write the two words that form the compound word on the lines.

1. He cleaned his teeth with a **toothpick**. ___tooth___ ___pick___

2. A **newspaper** has useful information. ___news___ ___paper___

3. He tripped on the crack in the **sidewalk**. ___side___ ___walk___

4. She gave a **haircut** to my mother. ___hair___ ___cut___

5. The police found a **fingerprint** on the door. ___finger___ ___print___

III. A vs. An

Directions: Fill in each blank with "a" or "an".

1. _A_ man in the park made _an_ elephant out of a balloon.

2. Karen wanted _an_ apple for _a_ snack.

3. Mrs. Smith is _a_ new teacher with _an_ easy class.

4. During the storm we need boots, _a_ rain coat, and _an_ umbrella.

5. There was _an_ emergency phone call from _a_ doctor.

Unit 8

Friendly Letters

Student

	Mastery	Non-Mastery
1. Friendly Letters		

Grammar Standards – Unit 8

Student

	Mastery	Non-Mastery
1. Friendly Letters		

Friendly Letters
#1

Below are two samples of how a friendly letter should look.

Heading	
Greeting,	
Body	
Closing,	
Signature	

1685 Main St. Downy, CA 90715 January 1, 2005
Dear Jennifer,
Guess what happened to me yesterday. I was at the mall. There was a booth set up for free make-overs. I got in line, and after an hour, it was my turn. The people there took my picture. They liked the picture so much that they're going to put it in a magazine. How exciting. I wonder what they meant by "a great 'before' picture". Write me back soon.
Sincerely, Erika

Notice the following:

1. The heading, closing, and signature all line up on the right.

2. There is a comma after the greeting and the closing.

3. The first paragraph of the body is indented. You follow all the rules of writing.

Your assignment:

Copy the "Dear Jennifer" letter from above on a separate sheet of paper.

Make sure that the heading, closing, and signature are all lined up.

Name: _____

Friendly Letters
#2

Headings

The heading of a friendly letter looks like this:

Address	555 Elm St.
City, State, Zip Code	Redding, CA 91343
Date	April 7, 2006

Directions: Put the headings from each box in the correct order. Write each one on the lines to the right.

1.
```
314 Clarke Ave.
December 15, 2000
Downey, CA 90801
```

_____

_____

_____

2.
```
5063 Fallin Ave.
Torrence, CA 90703
March 10, 2008
```

_____

_____

_____

3.
```
July 4, 1976
Philadelphia, PA 19103
333 Market Street
```

_____

_____

_____

4.
```
April 1, 2010
Phoenix, AZ 70812
333 Desert Rd.
```

_____

_____

_____

Extension: Select any two of the headings from above. Write them on a separate sheet of paper as if you were writing a real letter.

Friendly Letters #3

Below are two (2) one-sentence letters. Write them on the lines. Be sure the heading, closing, and signature all line up on the right. Put a comma after the greeting and the closing.

#1

5895 Ball Street / Lakewood, CA 90715 / January 1, 2004 / Dear Alice, Be sure to indent your paragraphs in the body of a letter. In this way you will have a good looking letter. / Yours truly, / Cindi Rella

_____

_____

_____

_____ ,

_____

_____

_____

_____

_____

#2

I got a bike today. What did you get? / 314 Main Street / Dear Mary, / Sincerely, / Joseph / Seal Beach, CA 90801 / December 25, 2000

_____

_____

_____

_____ ,

_____

_____

_____

_____

_____

Friendly Letters
#4

Directions: On a separate sheet of paper, rewrite the letters below. Be sure to put them in the proper order.

#1

July 4, 1776   /   333 Market Street   /   Philadelphia, Pennsylvania 19103   /

Do you still have my pen?   /   Sincerely,   /   Dear George,   /   Thomas

#2

May 12, 1863   /   284 Black Forest Lane   /   Torrance, CA 90503   /   Gretel   /

I ran out of bread crumbs. The nice lady in a house made of candy has some.

Meet us in the forest.   /   Your sister,   /   Dear Hansel,

#3

Dear Alex,   /   Thanks for the present. The poster will look great in my room. /

Bobby   /   2290 Foxhill Ave.   /   Sincerely,   /   October 12, 2004   /

Arlington, TX 76014

#4

My family will be leaving for Orlando, Florida tomorrow. We're going to visit

Disneyworld. I'll send you a postcard.   /   August 2, 2005   /   Dear Kelly,   /

258 Berry Street   /   Sacramento, CA 89581   /   Yours truly,   /   Pat Smith

#5

Harry   /   Sincerely,   /   I left my flying broom back in the closet . If you send

it to me here in America, I'll bring you some magic candy next summer.   /

Dear Dudley, / September 13, 2002 / New York, NY 10128 / 333 Castle Dr.

Friendly Letters
#5

Name: _____

Directions: On a separate sheet of paper, rewrite the letters below. Be sure to put them in the proper order.

#1

April 1, 2008   /   911 Beach Blvd.   /   Seattle, WA 98103   /   I'm staying here at camp for two more weeks. April Fools! See you on Saturday   /   Your son,   /   Dear Mom,   /   Ryan

#2

June 14, 1856   /   487 Jungle Rd.   /   Miami, FL 33125   /   Jane   /   Thank you for the lovely time in your jungle. I loved your tree house. Say hello to your animal friends.   /   Your friend,   /   Dear Tarzan,

#3

Dear Freddy,   /   How was your Christmas? Mine was great. I got a new bike and a new video game.   /   Billy   /   8544 Sugar Street   /   Sincerely,   /   December 25, 2004   /   Reno, NV 89502

#4

My family and I got to see the Space Shuttle land today. It was so exciting. We'll be in Yosemite tomorrow.   /   September 2, 2005   /   Dear Kyle,   /   912 Oak Ave.   /   Redding, CA 96003   /   Yours truly,   /   Michael Jones

#5

Marsha   /   Love,   /   Remember when you broke Mom's lamp? She always said not to play ball in the house.   /   Dear Peter,   /   May 30, 1972   /   Hollywood, CA 90068   /   621 Brady Lane

Extension: Write a letter to a friend. Be sure to use the correct format for letter writing.

Friendly Letters
Test

Directions: On a separate sheet of paper, write a letter to a friend. Use the information below for your heading. Be sure to follow all of the rules for letter writing.

*Heading: Today's Date   /   911 Beach Blvd.   /   Seattle, WA 98103

* Put these in the correct order.

Name: _____

Friendly Letters
Test

Directions: On a separate sheet of paper, write a letter to a friend. Use the information below for your heading. Be sure to follow all of the rules for letter writing.

*Heading: Today's Date   /   911 Beach Blvd.   /   Seattle, WA 98103

* Put these in the correct order.

Unit 9

Prefixes and Suffixes

Grammar Standards – Unit 9

_____
Student

	Mastery	Non-Mastery
1. Prefixes		
2. Suffixes		

Grammar Standards – Unit 9

_____
Student

	Mastery	Non-Mastery
1. Prefixes		
2. Suffixes		

Prefixes
#1

Name: _____

Main Idea: A prefix changes the **meaning** of a word.	

A prefix is a syllable added to **a base word** to change its meaning.

Example: "**un**" means not.   **un** + happy = not happy

I. Below are prefixes and their definitions. Add the prefix to the base word.
    Next, use the prefix to guess the definition of the <u>new word</u>. Use a
    dictionary to check your answers.

             Base Word   **New Word**   **New Definition**

1. **re = again**

        write - _____ - __**to write again**_____

        _____

        paint - _____ - _____

        _____

        take - _____ - _____

2. **un = not**

        fair - _____ - _____

        _____

        able - _____ - _____

        _____

        selfish - _____ - _____

3. **pre = before**

        test - _____ - _____

        _____

        school - _____ - _____

        _____

        pay - _____ - _____

Extension: Select one word from each prefix above. Write each one in
a sentence. Underline the prefix.

Prefixes
#2

I. Select a word from the box to complete each sentence.

1. Mom doesn't like the color so we need to _____ the house.	rewrite
2. Cindy thought getting a D on the test was _____.	repaint
3. Before going to kindergarten, I went to _____.	retake
4. If you are _____ you will share your crayons.	unfair
5. We revised our stories, and then we had to _____ them.	unable
6. The photographer had to _____ the picture.	unselfish
7. The new book comes out next year, but I can _____ now.	pretest
8. On Monday we take a spelling _____ before Friday's test.	preschool
9. If you're _____ to finish the math, ask for help.	prepay

II. Use a dictionary to look up two (2) words with the prefixes listed below. Write the **base word** on the line. Next, write the **base word** with the prefix together. Finally, write the definition of the word.

Note: When looking up the word, if there is no **base** word, it is not a prefix.

1. re – to do again   2. un = not   3. pre = before

Base Word   **Definition**

re - __work__ = __rework__ : _to do something over again to make it better_

re - _____ = _____ : _____

un - _____ = _____ : _____

un - _____ = _____ : _____

pre - _____ = _____ : _____

pre - _____ = _____ : _____

Prefixes
#3

Main Idea: A prefix changes the **meaning** of a word.

A prefix is a syllable added to **a base word** to change its meaning.

Example: "**un**" means not. **un** + happy = not happy

Directions: Add the prefix to the base word. Next, use the prefix to <u>guess the</u> <u>definition</u> of the <u>new word</u>. Use a dictionary to check your answers.

	Base Word	New Word	New Definition
1. bi = two			
	monthly -	_____	- _____
			_____
	annual -	_____	- _____
			_____
	weekly -	_____	- _____
2. mis = wrong			
	understand -	_____	- _____
			_____
	behave -	_____	- _____
			_____
	spell -	_____	- _____
3. dis = not			
	agree -	_____	- _____
			_____
	respect -	_____	- _____
			_____
	obey -	_____	- _____

Extension: Select one word from each prefix above. Write each one in a sentence. Underline the prefix.

Prefixes #4

Name: _____

I. Select a word from the box to complete each sentence.

1. Listen carefully so you don't _____ the assignment.

2. Use a dictionary so you don't _____ the word.

3. The _____ meeting happens in January and July.

4. Students who _____ the rules will have a timeout.

5. On the 1st and 16th he gets his _____ paycheck.

6. If you _____ you might lose a recess.

7. We are still friends even though we _____ constantly.

8. We have PE _____ on Tuesday and Thursday.

9. Don't show _____ to your parents by talking back.

bimonthly
biannual
biweekly
misunderstand
misbehave
misspell
disagree
disrespect
disobey

II. Use a dictionary to look up two (2) words with the prefixes listed below. Write the **base word** on the line. Next, write the **base word** with the prefix together. Finally, write the definition of the word.

Note: When looking up the word, if there is no **base** word, it is not a prefix.

1. bi – to   2. mis = wrong   3. dis = not

Base Word   **Definition**

bi - _____ = _____ : _____

bi - _____ = _____ : _____

mis - _____ = _____ : _____

mis - _____ = _____ : _____

dis - _____ = _____ : _____

dis - _____ = _____ : _____

Prefixes
#5

┌───┐
Other "Not" Prefixes

non -   im-   in-
└───┘

Main Idea: A prefix changes the _____ of a word.

I. Match the prefix from the box to each word below. Use a dictionary for help.

1. ____fat   4. ____balance   7. ____sensitive   10. ____stop

2. ____patient   5. ____fiction   8. ____mobile   11. ____perfect

3. ____secure   6. ____accurate   9. ____profit   12. ____expensive

II. Select a word from above to complete each sentence.

1. Because the toys were _____, we all bought one.

2. This is a true story so it is _____.

3. We took a _____ flight from Los Angeles to New York.

4. Calling someone names is very _____.

5. Mom had a _____ muffin because she's on a diet.

6. Bob broke his leg and was _____ for two weeks.

7. We can all go to the show because it is very _____.

8. Because we were so _____ we opened our presents last night.

9. You were _____ when you said two plus two is five.

10. We are all _____ and make mistakes all of the time.

Suffixes
#1

A **suffix** is a syllable added to the end of a word to <u>change its meaning</u>.

Main Idea: A suffix changes the **part of speech** of a word.

Examples:

sing = verb   sing<u>er</u> = noun   /   beauty = noun   beauti<u>ful</u> = adjective

---

Common Suffixes

1. -ful means "full of"   Example: color<u>ful</u> = full of color

2. -ous means "full of"   Example: fam<u>ous</u> = full of fame

3. -y means "full of"   Example: mess<u>y</u> = full of mess

4. -ible means "capable of"   Example: respons<u>ible</u> = capable of responding

5. -tion means "the act of"   Example: elec<u>tion</u> = the act of electing

6. -ive means "acting in a certain way"   Example: active = acting with action

7. -est means "greatest at"   Example: greatest = greatest at being great.

I. Select a suffix from the box that will change the meaning of each word below.

New Word	New Word
1. deep - __deepest__	9. add - _____
2. faith - _____	10. flex - _____
3. dirt - _____	11. impress - _____
4. nerve- _____	12. wonder - _____
5. sense- _____	13. taste - _____
6. migrate - _____	14. direct - _____
7. destruct - _____	15. big - _____
8. strong - _____	16. stick - _____

Suffixes
#2

Name: _____

Main Idea: A suffix changes the _____ ____ _____ of a word.

-ful	-able	-ous	-y	-ible	-tion	-ive	-est

I. Add the suffixes from the box to the words in parentheses to complete the following sentences:

1. After dinner, the table was _____.   (mess)

2. The _____ students were bothering the teacher.   (talk)

3. We all thought that the movie was very _____.   (enjoy)

4. She was a little _____ about singing on stage. (nerve)

5. My straight A's proves I'm the _____ in the class.   (smart)

6. The trash can was very _____.   (dirt)

7. Be careful because there may be a _____ snake around. (poison)

8. The flood caused the _____ of the city.   (destruct)

9. The waiter was very _____ not to spill the soup.   (care)

10. A _____ person would do all of his/her homework.   (response)

11. There was an _____ for class president.   (elect)

12. Because the back seat was _____, we could all fit in.   (space)

13. Susan is the _____ runner on the team.   (fast)

14. This cup is too _____ to use.   (dirt)

15. Amy did a _____ job on her test.   (miracle)

Extension: Select any five (5) words from the box above. Write them in sentences. Underline the suffix in each sentence.

Suffixes
#3

Main Idea: A suffix changes the _____ ____ _____ of a word.

Common Suffixes

1. -ful means "full of"   5. -tion means "the act of"

2. -ous means "full of"   6. -ive means "acting in a certain way"

3. -y means "full of"   7. -est means "greatest at"

4. -ible means "capable of"

I. The underlined word in the sentences below can be changed using suffixes.
   If you change the word using the suffix, then you need to change the sentence.

Directions: Rewrite each sentence below using the new word. There is
more than one way to write each sentence.

1. The stars in the sky were full of <u>wonder</u>.   (-ful)

    The stars in the sky were wonderful.

2. We were full of <u>nerves</u> because of the big test.   (-ous)

    _____

3. My shoes were full of <u>dirt</u>. (-y)

    _____

4. Heather can <u>create</u> many good pictures.   (-ive)

    _____

5. That soldier was the greatest at being <u>brave</u>.   (-est)

    _____

6. Andy has good <u>sense</u>. (-ible)

    _____

7. The birds will <u>migrate</u> this winter.   (-tion)

    _____

8. The actor is full of <u>fame</u>.   (-ous)

    _____

Suffixes
#4

Common "People" Suffixes

These suffixes all mean "a person that does something".

-er   -ar   -ist   -or

sing<u>er</u> – one who sings   li<u>ar</u> – one who lies   typ<u>ist</u> – one who types

supervis<u>or</u> – one who supervises

I. Change the words below into people by adding **-er -ar -ist -or** . Write the new word. Use a dictionary to check your answers.

1. drive - _____   7. help - _____

2. act - _____   8. instruct - _____

3. beg - _____   9. write - _____

4. cycle - _____   10. garden - _____

5. collect - _____   11. art - _____

6. geology - _____   12. aviation - _____

II. Write five sentences using the person and the action they do. See the sample below:

Example: The <u>driver</u> will <u>drive</u> to the park.

1. _____

2. _____

3. _____

4. _____

5. _____

Suffixes
#5

I. Change the words below into people by adding **-er -ar -ist -or**. Write the new word. Use a dictionary to check your answers.

1. dance - _____

9. play - _____

2. biology - _____

10. piano - _____

3. sail - _____

11. supervise - _____

4. lie - _____

12. guitar - _____

5. farm - _____

13. dance - _____

6. auth__ - _____

14. column - _____

7. dream - _____

15. select - _____

8. science - _____

16. doct___ - _____

II. Use the words on this page to write five sentences about a person and the action they do. See the sample below:

Example: The <u>driver</u> will <u>drive</u> to the park.

1. _____

2. _____

3. _____

4. _____

5. _____

Chapter 9
Review

I. Prefixes

A prefix changes the _____ of a word.

bi-	mis-	dis-	non-	im-	in-	re-	un-	pre-

Directions: Use a prefix from the box above to rewrite the underlined word.

_____ 1. To <u>paint</u> again

_____ 2. Not <u>fair</u>

_____ 3. School before <u>school</u>

_____ 4. Two times a <u>month</u>

_____ 5. To <u>behave</u> badly

_____ 6. To not <u>obey</u>

_____ 7. No <u>fat</u>

_____ 8. Not <u>perfect</u>

_____ 9. Not <u>expensive</u>

_____ 10. Not <u>happy</u>

II. Suffixes

A suffix changes the _____ ____ _____ of a word.

-ful	-able	-ous	-y	-er (person)	-tion	-ive	-est

Directions: Select a suffix from the box that will change the meaning of each word below. There may be more than one answer.

New Word

1. break - _____

2. create - _____

3. dirt - _____

4. wonder - _____

5. fame- _____

New Word

6. drive - _____

7. deep - _____

8. predict - _____

9. joy - _____

10. stop - _____

Name: _____

Chapter 9
Test

I. Prefixes

A prefix changes the _____ of a word.

bi- mis- dis- non- im- in- re- un- pre-

Directions: Use a prefix from the box above to rewrite the underlined word.

_____ 1. To not <u>respect</u>

_____ 2. Not <u>possible</u>

_____ 3. Two times a <u>week</u>

_____ 4. Not <u>selfish</u>

_____ 5. Not <u>secure</u>

_____ 6. To <u>write</u> again

_____ 7. Wrong <u>understanding</u>

_____ 8. Test before the <u>test</u>

_____ 9. To not <u>stop</u>

_____ 10. To <u>make</u> again

II. Suffixes

A suffix changes the _____ ____ _____ of a word.

-ful   -able   -ous   -y   -er (person)   -tion   -ive   -est

Directions: Select a suffix from the box that will change the meaning of each word below. There may be more than one answer.

New Word

1. enjoy - _____

2. poison - _____

3. care - _____

4. sing - _____

5. elect - _____

New Word

6. dirt - _____

7. miracle - _____

8. destruct - _____

9. kind - _____

10. wonder - _____

Chapter 9
Answer Key

I. Prefixes

A prefix changes the ___**meaning**___ of a word.

bi-	mis-	dis-	non-	im-	in-	re-	un-	pre-

Directions: Use a prefix from the box above to rewrite the underlined word.

**disrespect** 1. To not <u>respect</u>

**impossible** 2. Not <u>possible</u>

**biweekly** 3. Two times a <u>week</u>

**unselfish** 4. Not <u>selfish</u>

**insecure** 5. Not <u>secure</u>

**rewrite** 6. To <u>write</u> again

misunderstand 7. Wrong <u>understanding</u>

**pretest** 8. <u>Test</u> before the <u>test</u>

**nonstop** 9. To not <u>stop</u>

**remake** 10. To <u>make</u> again

II. Suffixes

A suffix changes the __**part**__ __**of**__ __**speech**__ of a word.

-ful	-able	-ous	-y	-er (person)	-tion	-ive	-est

Directions: Select a suffix from the box that will change the meaning of each word below. There may be more than one answer.

	New Word			New Word
1. enjoy -	**enjoyable**		6. dirt -	**dirty**
2. poison -	**poisonous**		7. miracle -	**miraculous**
3. care -	**careful**		8. destruct -	**destructive** / -ion
4. sing -	**singer**		9. kind -	**kindest**
5. elect -	**election** / **elective**		10. wonder -	**wonderful** / **wondrous**

Pg. 5 Nouns: Definitions #1
1. person　　2. place　　3. thing　　4. place　　5. thing　　6. person
7. thing　　8. place　　9. person　　10. place　　11. person　　12. thing

Pg. 6 Nouns: Definitions #2
A noun is the name of a person, place, or thing.
1. Sister Mary – proper / rings – common / Alejandra – proper / Juan – proper　　2. dog – common / Mrs. Ly –proper / neighbor – common　　3. family – common / San Francisco – proper / car – common / Golden Gate Bridge – proper
4. Simm's Park – proper / Halloween – proper (used as an adjective) / party – common / candy – common
5. Mrs. Jones – proper / class – common / pencils – common / paper – common / folders – common

Pg. 7 Nouns: Definitions #3
Common nouns do not name exact people, places, and things.　　Proper nouns name exact people, places and things.
Sections I and II - Answers will vary.
Section III – 1. common　　2. proper　　3. common　　4. proper　　5. proper　　6. common　　7. proper
　　　　　　8. common　　9. proper　　10. common

Pg. 8 Nouns: Definitions #4
Common nouns do not name exact people, places, and things.　　Proper nouns name exact people, places and things.
Sections I and II - Answers will vary.
Section III – 1. common　　2. common　　3. proper　　4. common　　5. proper　　6. proper　　7. common
　　　　　　8. proper　　9. proper　　10. common

Pg. 9 Nouns: Definitions #5
1. singular　　2. plural　　3. plural　　4. singular　　5. plural　　6. singular
7. singular　　8. plural　　9. singular　　10. plural　　11. plural　　12. singular

Pg. 10 Nouns: Definitions #6
Singular nouns name just one person, place, or thing.　　Plural nouns name more than one person, place, or thing.
1. singular　　2. plural　　3. singular　　4. singular　　5. plural　　6. plural　　7. singular
8. plural　　9. singular　　10. singular　　11. plural　　12. plural　　13. singular　　14. singular
15. plural　　16. plural　　17. singular　　18. plural　　19. plural　　20. singular

Pg. 11 Nouns: Definitions #7
Common nouns do not name exact people, places, and things.　　Proper nouns name exact people, places and things.
Singular nouns name just one person, place, or thing.　　Plural nouns name more than one person, place, or thing.

1. thing　　2. place　　3. person　　4. thing　　5. place　　6. person　　7. thing　　8. place

1. proper / singular　　2. common / plural　　3. common / plural　　4. proper / plural　　5. common / singular　6. common / plural　　7. proper / singular　　8. common / plural　　9. proper / singular　　10. common / singular

Pg. 12 Nouns: Possessive Nouns #1
1. John's book　　2. plane's wing　　3. bike's wheel　　4. door's handle　　5. Tom's friend　　6. room's light

Pg. 13 Nouns: Possessive Nouns #2
1. bees' hive　　2. friends' parents　　3. bikes' wheels　　4. planes' wings　　5. books' covers　　6. rooms' lights

1. men's room　　2. children's toy　　3. women's club　　4. deer's meadow　　5. geese's pond　　6. people's houses

Pg. 14 Nouns: Possessive Nouns #3
1. cow's bell / cows' bell　　2. child's toy / children's toy　　3. dog's bone / dogs' bone
4. man's sports / men's sports　　5. king's thoughts / kings' thoughts　　6. woman's purse / women's purse
7. bird's nest / birds' nest　　8. family's idea / families' idea

Pg. 15 Nouns: Possessive Nouns #4
A possessive noun owns, or possesses, another item.
1. Tim's yard   2. cities' houses   3. dishes' cupboard   4. farm's animals
5. actors' movie   6. children's play   7. Amy's friend   8. dresses' price
Part II – Answers will vary.

Pg. 16 Nouns: Possessive Nouns #5
A possessive noun owns, or possesses, another item.
1. lady's purse   2. sheep's wool   3. lab's computers   4. girls' ideas
5. bread's crust   6. students' game   7. brothers' puppy   8. horse's rider
Part II – Answers will vary.

Pg. 17-18 Nouns: Possessive Nouns #6-#7
Answers will vary.

Pg. 20 Nouns: Plural Nouns Rules #1 and #2
1. tries   2. hobbies   3. spies   4. countries   5. mysteries   6. beauties   7. cries   8. ladies

1. chimneys   2. birthdays   3. cowboys   4. donkeys   5. keys   6. toys   7. monkeys   8. bays

Pg. 21 Nouns: Plural Nouns Rules #1 and #2 Part II
Rule #1: If a word ends in "y", preceded by a consonant, change the "y" to "i" and add "es".
Rule #2: If a word ends in "y", preceded by a vowel, just add "s" to make the word plural.
1. #1 melodies   2. #2 cowboys   3. #1 skies   4. #1 copies   5. #2 chimneys   6. #2 donkeys   7. #1 flies
8. #2 toys   9. #1 countries 10. #1 hobbies 11. #2 birthdays 12. #1 injuries 13. #2 monkeys 14. #1 berries
15. #1 supplies 16. #2 bays   17. #1 mysteries 18. #1 spies   19. #2 keys   20. #1 ladies

Pg. 22 Nouns: Plural Nouns Rules #1 and #2 Part III
Answers will vary.

1. counties   2. injuries   3. cowboys   4. spies   5. bays   6. copies   7. beauties   8. melodies

Pg. 23 Nouns: Plural Nouns Rules #1 and #2 Quiz
1. hobbies   2. turkeys   3. berries   4. flies   5. birthdays   6. cowboys   7. injuries
8. copies   9. chimneys   10. valleys   11. cries   12. countries 13. mysteries 14. melodies
15. supplies 16. donkeys   17. spies   18. ladies   19. toys 20. beauties   21. skies   22. tries

Pg. 24 Nouns: Plural Nouns Rules #3 and #4
1. wolves   2. wives   3. beliefs   4. thieves   5. selves   6. calves   7. chiefs   8. lives   9. elves   10. shelves

1. banjos   2. potatoes   3. igloos   4. rodeos   5. tornadoes   6. buffaloes   7. tomatoes   8. solos   9. heroes   10. patios

Pg. 25 Nouns: Plural Nouns Rules #3 and #4 Part II
If a word ends in "f" or "fe", the "f" or "fe" is usually changed to "v", and "es" is added to make the word plural. Chief and
belief are two exceptions.   /   If a word ends in "o", just "s" is added to make the word plural. Some words add "es".

1. #3 leaves   2. #4 heroes   3. #3 wolves   4. #4 patios   5. #4 buffaloes   6. #3 knives   7. #3 selves
8. #4 banjos   9. #4 tomatoes 10. #3 halves 11. #4 rodeos   12. #3 thieves   13. #4 solos   14. #4 tornadoes
15. #3 loaves 16. #3 lives   17. #4 photos 18. #4 potatoes 19. #3 shelves   20. #2 pianos

Pg. 26 Nouns: Plural Nouns Rules #3 and #4 Part III
Answers will vary.

1. halves   2. banjos   3. wolves   4. tomatoes   5. patios   6. wives   7. solos   8. rodeos

Pg. 27 Nouns: Plural Nouns Rules #3 and #4 Quiz
1. calves   2. pianos   3. potatoes   4. wives   5. loaves   6. rodeos   7. wolves   8. thieves
9. patios   10. selves   11. heroes   12. lives   13. tornadoes   14. halves   15. banjos   16. leaves
17. igloos   18. buffaloes 19. elves   20. tomatoes 21. shelves   22. photos   23. knives   24. solos

Pg. 28 Nouns: Plural Nouns Rules #5 and #6
1. geese   2. churches   3. branches   4. deer   5. guesses   6. oxen   7. foxes
8. sheep   9. lunches   10. children   11. teeth   12. glasses   13. crutches   14. mice

Pg. 29 Nouns: Plural Nouns Rules #5 and #6   Part II
Some words form their plurals in unusual ways.   /   If a word ends in "ss", "x", "z", "sh", or "ch" the suffix "es" is usually added to make the word plural.

1. #5 sheep   2. #6 patches   3. #5 men   4. #6 flashes   5. #5 oxen   6. #6 punches   7. #6 guesses
8. #5 children   9. #6 lunches   10. #6 foxes   11. #5 teeth   12. #5 deer   13. #6 churches   14. #5 women
15. #6 branches   16. #5 geese   17. #6 glasses   18. #5 feet   19. #6 taxes   20. #5 mice

Pg. 30 Nouns: Plural Nouns Rules #5 and #6   Part III
1. sheep   2. punches   3. feet   4. taxes   5. teeth   6. waltzes   7. children   8. branches

Pg. 31 Nouns: Plural Nouns Rules #5 and #6   Quiz
1. taxes   2. women   3. crutches   4. punches   5. touches   6. mice   7. feet   8. buzzes   9. deer
10. lunches   11. glasses   12. patches   13. teeth   14. guesses   15. oxen   16. sheep   17. waltzes   18. foxes
19. hunches   20. men   21. bunches   22. geese   23. flashes   24. churches   25. children   26. branches

Pg. 32 Noun Review #1
Common nouns do not name exact people, places, and things.   Proper nouns name exact people, places and things.
Singular nouns name just one person, place, or thing.   Plural nouns name more than one person, place, or thing.
A possessive noun owns, or possesses, another item.
1. doctor's – singular, common, possessive   2. Jeff – singular, proper   3. cows – plural, common
4. New York's – singular, proper, possessive   5. flower – singular, common   6. rocks – plural, common
7. brother's – plural, common, possessive   8. road – singular, common   9. Arizona's – singular, proper, possessive
10. Ms. Daisy – singular, proper   11. clowns – plural, common   12. baskets – plural, common
13. hammers' – plural, common, possessive   14. sun – singular, common   15. Anna's – singular, proper, possessive

Pg. 33 Noun Review #2
1. Mt. Hood – singular, proper   2. Mike's – singular, proper, possessive   3. spoons – plural, common
4. children's – plural, common, possessive   5. Great Lakes – plural, proper   6. ducks' – plural, common, possessive
7. game – singular, common   8. Play Station – singular, proper   9. teachers' – plural, common, possessive
10. cities – plural, common

1. neighbor's cabin   2. desert's flower   3. stories' author   4. farm's animals   5. actors' movie   6. friends' feelings

1. cities   2. churches   3. solos   4. toys   5. lives   6. guesses   7. flies   8. monkeys   9. selves

Pg. 41 Capitalization: Common and Proper Nouns #1
1. common – dog – thing   2. proper – Mt. Wilson – place   3. common – street – place   4. common – beaver – thing
5. proper – Texas – place   6. proper - Snake River – place   7. common – island – place   8. common – banana – thing
9. common – teacher – person   10. proper – Mr. Dean - person

Pg. 42 Capitalization: Common and Proper Nouns #2
1. common – home – place   2. proper – Pacific Ocean – place   3. proper – Dr. Drew – person
4. common – pizza – thing   5. common – bank – place   6. common – circus – place   7. proper – Olympics – thing
8. common – principal – person   9. proper – Mars – place   10. common – pencil – thing   11. proper – Mexico – place
12. common – clock – thing

Pg. 43 Capitalization: Common and Proper Nouns #3
C Lake / P Lake Tahoe – GN   C city / P Bellflower – GN   P Jurassic Period - HP / C year
P Sacramento - GN / C capital   C spring / P Impressionist Period – HP   C planet / P Pluto – GN
P Renaissance – HP / C decade   P Yosemite – GN / C park   P Mexico – GN / C country
P Age of Exploration – HP / C century

Pg. 44 Capitalization: Common and Proper Nouns #4
1. Independence Day – Holiday   2. Lindstrom's Talent Show – Special Event   3. Arbor Day – Holiday
4. Rose Parade – Special Event   5. Valentine's Day – Holiday   6. Beth Temple Bake Sale – Special Event
7. Memorial Day – Holiday   8. Thanksgiving – Holiday   9. Opening Day – Special Event
10. Labor Day – Holiday   11. Kentucky Derby – Special Event   12. Christmas – Holiday
13. Olympics – Special Event   14. Lakewood's Firework Spectacular – Special Event

Pg. 45 Capitalization: Common and Proper Nouns #5
1. P – Central Valley   2. C – birthday   3. P - St. Patrick's Day   4. C – space   5. P – Hanukkah   6. C – soda
7. P – Snake River   8. C – mountain   9. P – Iron Age   10. P – Black History Month   11. C – space shuttle
12. P – Opening Day   13. C – party   14. P – Halloween

Pg. 46 Capitalization: Common and Proper Nouns #6
1. P – New York   2. P – First Communion   3. C – parade   4. P – Ice Age   5. P – New Year's Eve
6. C – midnight   7. P – California   8. C – river   9. P – Easter   10. P – Thanksgiving

Pg. 47 Capitalization: Common and Proper Nouns #7
1. Proper – Grand Canyon   2. Common – river   3. Common – moon   4. Common – state   5. Proper – Pizza Hut
6. Proper – Jupiter   7. Common – mountain   8. Proper – Jimmy   9. Proper – Roget's Dictionary
10. Common – Kickball   11. Proper – Grand Canyon   12. Proper – Florida   13. Common – orange juice
14. Common – cake   15. Proper – World War II   16. Common – egg

Common Nouns: surprise, birthday, week, bed, morning, mountain, presents, dinning room, table, heart, movies, freeway, mountain, ride, sky, park, friends, presents, hands, smiles, faces, cousin, costumes, surprise, rides, day, time, home, birthday.
Proper Nouns: Mom, Dad, Renaissance Fair, Bugs Bunny Film Festival, Empire State Building, Chevy Suburban, Golden State Freeway, Matterhorn, Disneyland, Randy, Helen, Michael, Lisa, Skeeter, Medieval Period, Space Mountain, Big Thunder Mountain, The Haunted Mansion

Pg. 48 Capitalization: Common and Proper Nouns #8
Old West, The Licorice Kid, New Mexico, Texas, Buttercup, The Licorice Kid, Albuquerque, Pokemon Pete, Pete, Sunflower Park, The Licorice Kid, Pete, Kid, Jose, Tickle-Me-Elmo, Levis, Pokemon Pete, Charizard, Kid, Pokemon Pete, Pokemon, The Licorice Kid, Wells Fargo, California, Sacramento, Albuquerque

Pg. 49 Capitalization: Common and Proper Nouns Test Review
1. Proper – California – Place – GN   2. Proper – Pacific Ocean – Place – GN   3. Common – doctor – person
4. Proper - World War II – Thing – HP   5. Common – city – Place   6. Proper – San Diego – Place – GN
7. Common – pencil – Thing   8. Proper – Black History Month – Thing – SE
9. Proper – Miss America Pageant – Thing – SE   10. Common – alligator – Thing   11. Common – computer – Thing
12. Proper – New Year's Eve – Thing – H   13. Common – bridge – Thing   14. Common – camera – Thing
15. Proper – Kentucky Derby – Thing - SE

Pg. 55 Parts of Speech Ch.3 Study Sheet
Pronouns take the place of a **noun**. Examples: he or **him, they** or them, hers
Three kinds of **verbs**: 1. Action Words - Examples: run, jump, hit   2. "To Be" Words – Examples: is, am, are   3. Helping Verbs: can, should, has
Adjectives describe a **noun** or a **pronoun**. Answer: What kind? Big How Many? Three How Much? Several

Pg. 56 Pronouns #1
9 John's and 9 Tina's

Pg. 57 Pronouns #2
1. Mr. Saito – he, him, his   2. Rachel and Molly – They, them, theirs   3. Candice - she, her, hers   4. our class – we, us, ours   5. I, me, mine   6. pencil – it   7. Tammy and ___ - we, us, ours   8. football players – they, them, theirs
9. book – it   10. coaches – they, them, theirs   11. Mrs. Morrison – she, her, hers   12. you / best friend – we, us, ours

Pg. 58 Pronouns #3
A pronoun takes the place of a noun.
1. She gave it to her.   2. It chased them.   3. They gave it to them.   4. She baked them for us.   5. We snuck them into it.
6. He sent their* clothes to her.   7. He made them run laps around it.   8. They traveled with her to his* ranch.
* Technically an adjective acting as a pronoun.

Pg. 59 Pronouns #4
A pronoun takes the place of a noun.
1. He built it for him, and he really liked it.   2. We read it to them.   3. Their* grades were better than her* grades.
4. He sent it to him by mistake.   5. Making them sing it is like making it fly.   6. Her* joke made them laugh so they retold it.
7. This is his* book so put it where he can find it.   8. They let them join it.   9. It showed them bouncing it on their* noses.
10. They play them, but we can't see it.

Pg. 60 Pronouns #5
Answers will vary.

Pg. 61 Pronouns #6
They / their / it / I / you / your* / them / he / them / her* / they / them / we / them / us /
he / we / them / them / our* / their* / her / she / it / her* / it / hers / it / it / her* / she

Pg. 62 Verbs #1
I. Answers will vary.   II. 1. gave   2. run   3. want   4. waited   5. was / brought   6. are camping

Pg. 63 Verbs #2
A verb shows **action**.   Parts I and II – Answers will vary.

Pg. 64 Verbs #3
1. talked / talk / will talk   2. walked / walk / will walk   3. knew / know / will know   4. looked / look / will look
5. spoke / speak / will speak   6. arrived / arrive / will arrive   7. sat / sit / will sit   8. taught / teach / will teach

1. present / future / past   2. past / present / future   3. present / future / past   4. past / present / future
5. present / future / past   6. future / past / present

Pg. 65 Verbs #4
1. sang / sing / will sing   2. thought / think / will think   3. loved / love / will love   4. typed / type / will type
5. fought / fight / will fight   6. left / leave / will leave   7. hit / hit / will hit   8. sailed / sail / will sail

1. present / future   2. past / present   3. present / future   4. present / past   5. past / future   6. future / past

Pg. 66 Verbs #5
1. am   2. are / were   3. are / were   4. is / was   5. are / were   6. was   7. am   8. was   9. was   10. is / was

Pg. 67 Verbs #6
Answers will vary.

Pg. 68 Verbs #7
I. Answers will vary.
II. 1. Helping – is asking   2. To Be – was   3. Helping – is making   4. To Be – am   5. Helping – was singing
   6. To Be – were   7. Helping - are making   8. To Be – was

Pg. 69 Verbs #8
1. Action – made   2. To Be – is   3. Helping – were complaining   4. Action – drove   5. Helping – am making
6. Action – wrestled   7. To Be - is   8. To Be – was   9. Helping – were ready   10. Action – wrote
11. Helping – is looking   12. Helping – will drink

Pg. 70 Adjectives #1
1. What kind?   2. How many?   3. How many?   4. How many?   5. What kind?   6. What kind?   7. What kind?
8. What kind?   9. What kind?   10. How much?

Part II – Answers will vary

Pg. 71 Adjectives #2
1. What kind?   2. How many?   3. How many?   4. How many?   5. What kind?   6. What kind?   7. What kind?
8. What kind?   9. What kind?   10. How much?

Part II – Answers will vary

Pg. 72-73 Adjectives #3 - #4
Answers will vary.

Pg. 74 Adjectives #5
1. more intelligent / most intelligent   2. bigger / biggest   3. calmer / calmest   4. more powerful / most powerful
5. messier / messiest   6. darker / darkest   7. more exciting / most exciting   8. riskier / riskiest
9. more curious / most curious   10. angrier / angriest   11. smaller / smallest   12. more dangerous / most dangerous

Pg. 75 Adjectives #6
1. better / best   2. newer / newest   3. more intelligent / most intelligent   4. more patient / most patient
5. grouchier / grouchiest   6. cheaper / cheapest   7. more patriotic / most patriotic   8. dumpier / dumpiest
All of the words that end in Y, the Y is changed to "i".

1. Superlative – darkest   2. Comparative – tastier   3. Superlative – cleanest   4. Comparative – better
5. Superlative – funniest   6. Comparative – more dangerous   7. Comparative – more surprising   8. Superlative – nicest

Pg. 76 Adjectives #7
I. Answers will vary.   II. 1. strongest   2. older   3. messier   4. most exciting   5. cheaper
6. most dangerous animal   7. cooler   8. most intelligent

Pg. 77 Contractions #1
1. he would   2. they are   3. I am   4. you will   5. we are
6. are not   7. do not   8. it will   9. should have   10. has not

1. he'll   2. they've   3. haven't   4. we'll   5. it's   6. couldn't   7. I've   8. she's   9. won't   10. can't

Pg. 78 Contractions #2
1. he's / he'd / he'd / he'll   2. they'll / they're / they'd / they'd / they've   3. I'm / I've / I'll / I'd
4. you've / you're / you'll / you'd / you'd   5. we'll / we're / we'd / we'd / we've   6. couldn't / could've
7. it'll / it's   8. should've / shouldn't   9. wouldn't / would've   10. don't   11. won't   12. aren't
13. hasn't   14. didn't   15. haven't

Pg. 79 Contractions #3
1. cannot – can't   2. will not – won't   3. cannot – can't or will not – won't   4. will not – won't   5. cannot – can't
6. will not – won't   7. cannot – can't   8. will not – won't   9. cannot – can't   10. will not – won't

1. Amy is   2. John will   3. cannot   4. they are   5. you have
6. will not   7. has not   8. I am   9. would have   10. we are

Pg. 80 Contractions #4
1. We don't need to bring anything to the party.   2. Hazel won't let anybody ride her bike.   3. He can't ever make that work.   4. The police wouldn't let any cars go into the lot.   5. This game doesn't ever work properly.   6. My sister isn't ever ready on time.   7. He didn't want any olives on his pizza.   8. Dad won't let anyone use his camera again.

Pg. 81 Contractions #5
I. Answers will vary.
II. 1. he'll   2. they've   3. won't   4. they'd   5. weren't   6. I'll   7. they're   8. can't   9. you're   10. don't

Pg. 82 Contractions #6
I. Answers will vary.
II. 1. he will   2. they would   3. has not   4. cannot   5. do not
6. there is   7. will not   8. could have   9. I am   10. were not

Pg. 83-84 Chapter 3 Review
A pronoun takes the place of a noun.
I. 1. She gave it to her. 2. He made them for us. 3. They let them have it. 4. She gave his* book to him.
5. We played checkers with them. 6. We borrowed her* chairs for the party.
II.
1. sang / sing / will sing 2. thought / think / will think 3. read / read / will read 4. typed / type / will type
5. fought / fight / will fight

III. A. Answers will vary. B. 1. better / best 2. more intelligent / most intelligent

IV. A. 1. can't 2. won't 3. you've 4. you're 5. isn't 6. it's
B. 1. The camera didn't have any film in it. 2. We won't ever get there.

Pg. 91 Comma Rules: Dates #1
A. March 3, 2008 B. October 2007 C. December 25, 2000 D. January 1, 2010 E. April 8, 1841
F. May 2005 G. November 25, 2002 H. February 2012 I. October 31, 2007 J. August 2004
K. December 31, 1999 L. March 5, 2005 M. June 28, 1824 N. May 18, 2006 O. July 2015

Pg. 92 Comma Rules: Dates #2
A. March 3, 2008 B. October 2007 C. December 25, 2000 D. June 27, 2004 E. September 1, 1986
F. February 1922 G. August 2009 H. January 4, 2005 I. March 9, 2007 J. April 30, 1845
K. May 1776 L. July 4, 1776

December 15, 2000 / January 16, 2001 / February 17, 2002 / March 18, 1973 / April 1974 / May 2004 /
June 2005 / July 19, 2005 / August 20, 1974

Pg. 93 Comma Rules: City, State / Addresses #1
A. Los Angeles, California B. 321 Main Street, Orange, Florida C. 11408 E. 211th, Tulane, OH D. Miami, Florida
E. Sacramento, California F. 241 Jersey Way, Denver, Colorado G. 949 Arbor St. Franklin, TN H. Houston, Texas
I. Portland, Oregon J. 3305 Lees Ave., Atlanta, Georgia K. 13 Big St. , Kona, Hawaii L. Las Vegas, Nevada

Pg. 94 Comma Rules: City, State / Addresses #2
A. Boise, Idaho B. 14732 Bowling Lane, Chicago, Illinois C. 484 East St., Augusta, Maine
D. Minneapolis, Minnesota E. Lincoln, Nebraska F. 15243 West Point, Albany, New York
G. 9185 Main Ave., Toledo, OH H. Hershey, Pennsylvania I. Salt Lake City, Utah J. 22448 Kite St. Helena, Montana

Springfield, Missouri / 327 Viking Way, Galloway, Missouri / Flagstaff, Arizona / San Antonio, Texas /
323 Heart St., Bellflower, California / 4545 Henrilee Ave., Lawton, Oklahoma

Pg. 95 Comma Rules: Mixed Review
1. April 22, 2004 / Honolulu, Hawaii 2. none 3. April 5, 2003 / 4531 E. Arlington Rd., Dallas, Texas
4. May 3, 1920 / San Diego, CA / Long Island, New York 5. 222 Washington Rd., Seal Beach, CA
6. 123 Gum Drop Lane, North Pole, Alaska 7. Atlanta, Georgia / February 2, 2010
8. 396 Big Bear Ave., Arrowhead, CA

1. October 31, 2010 2. Brooklyn, New York 3. 1314 Love Ave. Lakewood, Colorado 4. no comma
5. August 12, 2008 6. 555 Hope Ave. Little Rock, Arkansas

Pg. 96 Comma Rules: Lists #1
1. We learned about the moon, stars, and planets in science. 2. There are scissors, crayons, and pencils on your table.
3. It seems like we read, write, and study all day. 4. Amy, Sally, and Melissa are best friends.
5. Mom told me to wash, rinse, and dry the dishes. 6. The store was out of chocolate, vanilla, and strawberry ice cream.
7. Our new puppy has chewed up my slippers, socks, dolls, and homework. 8. We put milk, butter, sugar, and flour into the recipe. 9. David, Joy, Shawn, and Ryan are on the same team. 10. My mom's favorite holidays are Christmas, Easter, 4th of July, and Thanksgiving. 11. We need to put spoons, knives, and forks on the table.
12. Leaves, twigs, and trash blew onto our yard. 13. Johnny has a fish, dog, mouse, and lizard for a pet.
14. The show will start when the teachers, students, and parents enter. 15. Our team needs a new pitcher, catcher, and captain.

Pg. 97 Comma Rules: Lists #2
1. The story was about how a bird, mouse, and snake became friends.   2. The sun causes wind, rain, hurricanes, and tornadoes.   3. Police, fire-fighters, and paramedics participated in the assembly.   4. We need glue, scissors, and tissue for our art project.   5. Washington, Adams, and Jefferson were our first presidents.   6. My dad is afraid of snakes, spiders, and mice.   7. Today I wrote, revised, and edited my report.   8. Her baby brother likes to be tickled on his belly, feet, and chin.   9. Mr. Alexander taught us about health, science, and history.
10. Along the beach were sand castles children and seaweed.

Pg. 98 Comma Rules: Lists #3
Answers will vary.

Pg. 99 Comma Rules: Adjectives #1
1. There were many bright, colorful lights around the tree.   2. The strong, brave workers saved the girl from the burning building.   3. We walked into the room and saw short, busy elves making toys.
4. All the girls were wearing long, clean, colorful dresses.   5. The whining, complaining children were ready for a nap.   6. We used our tongues to lick the sweet, sticky syrup from our mouths.
7. The clown's thick, curly, colorful hair made him look funny.
8. Amy has small, fuzzy animals all over her bed.   9. Many hungry, dirty lumberjacks came into the restaurant.   10. Captain Hook was a mean, nasty, cheating, no-good, worthless pirate.

Pg. 100 Comma Rules: Adjectives #2
11.   We worked for two long, hard hours on this puzzle.   2. Our new neighbors have two nice, cheerful children.   3. Mom said it was time to throw away these old, dirty shirts.   4. The dark, flat clouds made their way across the sky.   5. Her tiny, broken umbrella couldn't keep the cold, sharp rain away.
6. The young, handsome soldiers marched in the parade.   7. The song had a fun, bouncy sound to it.
8. Yvette has such long, dark, beautiful hair.   9. The long, boring game seemed to last forever.
10. The wild, crazy boys destroyed the room.

Pg. 101 Comma Rules: Adjectives #3
Answers will vary.

Pg. 102 Comma Rules: Friendly Letter #1
1. Dear Nemo, - Greeting / Sincerely, - Closing   2. Dear Shrek, - Greeting / Your friend, - Closing
3. Dear Belle, - Greeting / Truly yours, - Closing   4. Dear Woody, - Greeting / Best wishes, - Closing
5. Dear Sulley, - Greeting / Your friend, – Closing

Pg. 103 Comma Rules: Friendly Letter #3
1. Dear Mrs. Clause, - Greeting / Sincerely, – Closing   2. Dear Captain Hook, - Greeting / Your friend, – Closing   3. Dear Pumba, - Greeting / Your buddy, – Closing

Pg. 105 Comma Rules: Mixed Review #1
1. There was a wild**,** exciting party on January 1**,** 2004. **Adjectives / Day, Year**
2. San Francisco, California, is famous for earthquakes, hills, houses, and bridges. **City-State / Lists**
3. Dear Porky,   In April 2012 meet me outside your house with a bottle of ketchup.   **Greeting**
     Your friend, B.B. Wolf   **Closing**
4. A soft, cuddly bunny will enjoy a carrot, radish, or lettuce.   **Adjective / Lists**
5. Williamsburg, Virginia was a big crowded city on July 4, 1776.   **City-State / Day-Year**
6. Dear Mickey,   You have the cutest, large round ears.   **Greeting / Adjectives**
     Sincerely,   Minnie   **Closing**
7. On May 19, 1968, the moon, earth, and sun lined up.   **Day-Year / Lists**
8. A large, hairy spider was found at 222 W. Palm Dr. in Miami, Florida.   **Adjectives / City-State**

Pg. 106 Comma Rules: Mixed Review #2
1. My dad proposed to my mom in Lincoln, Nebraska on February 14, 2000.   **City-State / Day-Year**
2. Dear, Martha   The soldiers just loved the biscuits, gravy, and jam.   **Greeting / Lists**
     Love,   George W.   **Closing**

Pg. 106 Comma Rules: Mixed Review #2 (cont.)

3. There was a concert in Denver, Colorado in December 2001.   **City-State**
4. Mail the coupon to 293 Broadway, Mobile, Alabama, for a free prize, picture, and autograph. **Address/Lists**
5. The fastest, strongest wolf usually becomes the leader of the pack.   **Adjectives**
6. Dear Thomas,   My new address is 484 Eastern St., Brain Tree, Massachusetts.   **Greeting / City-State**
   Sincerely,   John   **Closing**
7. The silly, entertaining clown wore a funny hat, shoes, and pants.   **Adjectives**
8. Parents can send post cards, presents, and treats to their children at 11934 Pine Ave., Crestline, California. **Lists / City-State**

Pg. 107 Comma Rules: Mixed Review #3

1. The address on the birthday invitation said 427 Stevely, Branson, Iowa   **City-State**
2. She had cookies, cake, and ice cream at her party.   **Lists**
3. Old cartoons ended in December 2004, but started again on January 3, 2004.   **Day-Year**
4. This summer we're going to St. Louis, Missouri.   **City-State**
5. Mom put a large, fluffy pancake on my plate.   **Adjectives**
6. Dear Rabbit,   You have such a beautiful, peaceful garden. **Greeting / Adjectives**
      Yours truly,   Pooh   **Closing**
7. We love to run, jump, and slide in the snow.   **Lists**
8. My first house was 724 Ram St., Tulsa, Oklahoma.   **City-State**
9. Is the happiest place on earth Anaheim, California or Orlando, Florida.   **City-State**
10. The Super Bowl was on February 6, 2005   **Day-Year**

Pg. 108 Comma Rules: Mixed Review #4

1. The beautiful, ancient tradition of Chanukah began on December 8, 2004.   **Adjectives / Day-Year**
2. The furniture, clothes, and dishes will be delivered to 374 Main St, Richmond, Virginia. **Lists / City-State**
3. Dear Ariel, Do you give singing lessons? You have such an amazing, angelic voice. **Greeting / Adjectives**
   Sincerely yours,   E. Fudd   **Closing**
4. There were floats, bands, and horses at the New Year's Day Parade on January 1, 2003. **Lists / Day-Year**
5. Brilliant, hard-working scientists predict that there will be a colony on Mars by December 2050. **Adjectives**
6. Dear Mr. Troll,   Sorry about that whole bridge thing. I hope your head feels better.   **Greeting**
Yours truly,   Bill Goat   **Closing**

Pg. 113 Four Types of Sentences #1

1. Interrogative – Where are you going?   2. Declarative – I'm going to the store.
3. Declarative – There's a sale on shirts.   4. Interrogative – How much are the shirts?
5. Declarative – You can get two shirts for $15.

Pg. 114 Four Types of Sentences #2

1. Declarative   2. Interrogative   3. Declarative   4. Declarative   5. Interrogative
6. Interrogative   7. Declarative   8. Declarative   9. Interrogative   10. Declarative

Pg. 115 Four Types of Sentences #3

1. Imperative   2. Exclamatory   3. Exclamatory   4. Imperative   5. Imperative

Pg. 116 Four Types of Sentences #4

1. Exclamatory   2. Imperative   3. Exclamatory   4. Imperative   5. Imperative
6. Exclamatory   7. Exclamatory   8. Imperative   9. Imperative   10. Exclamatory

Pg. 117 Four Types of Sentences #5

1. Interrogative   2. Declarative   3. Exclamatory   4. Imperative   5. Exclamatory
6. Interrogative   7. Declarative   8. Exclamatory   9. Imperative   10. Declarative   11. Interrogative

Pg. 118 Four Types of Sentences #6
1. Imperative   2. Declarative   3. Exclamatory   4. Interrogative   5. Imperative   6. Declarative
7. Imperative   8. Declarative   9. Interrogative   10. Exclamatory   11. Exclamatory   12. Interrogative

Pg. 121 Subjects #1
1. who   2. what   3. what   4. who   5. what   6. who   7. what   8. what   9. who   10. what

1. Mrs. Garcia   2. pencil   3. ice   4. girl   5. tree   6. bird   7. Dad   8. hammer   9. button   10. Mom

Pg. 122 Subjects #2
1. what   2. who   3. what   4. who   5. who   6. what   7. who   8. who   9. what   10. what

1. radio – what   2. music – what   3. Mr. Jones – who   4. concert – what   5. wrestler – who
6. crowd – who   7. love – what   8. room – what   9. paper – what   10. you – who

Pg. 123 Subjects #3
1. who   2. what   3. what   4. what   5. who   6. what   7. who   8. what   9. what   10. who

1. he – who   2. party – what   3. fork – what   4. It – what   5. doll – what
6. bed – what   7. dollar – what   8. ride – what   9. memory – what   10. Jay – who

Pg. 124 Predicates #1
1. Subject - ___ / Predicate = is – is   2. Subject – Mrs. Garcia / Predicate = is – is   3. Subject - tree / Predicate = is – is
4. Subject - tree / Predicate = is – is   5. Subject - teacher / Predicate = gave – does
6. Subject - teacher / Predicate = gave – does   7. Subject - leaves / Predicate = were – is
8. Subject - leaves / Predicate = were – is

Pg. 125 Predicates #2   Simple Predicate in Bold
1. **made** caramel apples – does   2. **am** sorry about the broken glass - is   3. **pulled** the nails across the table – does
4. **is** hungry – is   5. **played** on the grass – does   6. **rang** at the end of recess   7. **were** leaders of student council – is
8. **are** good helpers during the holidays – is   9. **are** good workers – is   10. **found** a safe place to park during the storm – does

Pg. 126 Predicates #3   Simple Predicate in Bold
1. **rode** the pony all morning – does   2. **is** an expert rider – is   3. **broke** down – does   4. **are** happy about walking to
school – is   5. **drove** down the street – does   6. **are** happy with their children   7. **is** king of the jungle
8. **threw** small, rubber spiders in our laps – does   9. **was** ready to start – is   10. **sang** a song about friends – does
11. **are** winners of the game – is   12. **were** good sports – is

Pg. 127 Finding Subjects and Predicates #1
1. predicate   2. subject   3. predicate   4. subject   5. predicate
6. subject   7. predicate   8. predicate   9. predicate   10. subject

Pg. 128 Finding Subjects and Predicates #2
1. predicate   2. subject   3. predicate   4. predicate   5. subject
6. predicate   7. subject   8. subject   9. predicate   10. subject

Pg. 129 Finding Subjects and Predicates #3
1. subject – frog / C.P. - jumped into the water.   2. subject – fish / C.P. - is in the pond.
3. subject – spiders / C.P. - live under that rock.   4. subject – I / C.P. -am tired of washing the dog.
5. subject – fly / C.P. - buzzed around my ear.   6. subject – cow / C.P. - was in the field.
7. subject – bears / C.P. - protect their cubs.   8. subject – eggs / C.P. - hatch in the sand.
9. subject – birds / C.P. - are wet because of the rain.   10. subject – tail / C.P. - broke off.
11. subject – toucan / C.P. - is yellow and red with orange feathers.
12. subject – butterflies / C.P. - are on the grass.

Pg. 130 Finding Subjects and Predicates #4
1. subject – cheetahs / C.P. - are faster than zebras.   2. subject – fish / C.P. - glistened in the light.
3. subject – snake / C.P. - rested on a rock in the warm sun.   4. subject – mouse / C.P. - tricks the cat always.
5. subject – kittens / C.P. - waited for their mother.   6. subject – scarecrow / C.P. - scared away the birds.

Pg. 130 Finding Subjects and Predicates #4   (cont.)

7. subject – turkey / C.P. - wants to fly.   8. subject – horses / C.P. - galloped across the field.

9. subject – dog / C.P. – is strong   10. subject – worms / C.P. - are good diggers.

11. subject – lizard / C.P. - climbed the wall.   12. subject – dog / C.P. - ate my homework.

Pg. 131-132 Chapter 5 Review #1

1. Declarative   2. Interrogative   3. Imperative   4. Exclamatory   5. Imperative   6. Interrogative
7. Exclamatory   8. Declarative

1. what   2. who   3. who   4. what   5. who   6. what   7. what   8. who

Part B – 1. is – are the champions   2. does – flows across my grandpa's farm   3. does – played on the swings during recess.
4. is – were tired after the game.   5. does – fell on our heads

1. Simple Subject – paint / Predicate – spilled out of the cup   2. Simple Subject – flowers / Predicate – are in the garden
3. Simple Subject – bats / Predicate – hang from the top of caves   4. Simple Subject – dog / Predicate – barked at the cat for
an hour   5. Simple Subject – class / Predicate – is best   6. Simple Subject – spiders / Predicate – spin beautiful webs
7. Simple Subject – Cindy / Predicate – drank all of the juice   8. Simple Subject – she / Predicate – was late for dinner

Pg. 133-134 Chapter 5 Review #2

1. Interrogative   2. Imperative   3. Exclamatory   4. Declarative   5. Exclamatory   6. Interrogative
7. Declarative   8. Imperative

1. who   2. what   3. who   4. what   5. what   6. who   7. who   8. what

Part B - 1. does – fly south for the winter   2. is – is a teacher   3. is – were ready for a bone
                4. does – threw darts at balloons.   5. does – find food in the weirdest places

1. Simple Subject – paint / Predicate – spilled out of the cup   2. Simple Subject – flowers / Predicate – are in the garden
3. Simple Subject – bats / Predicate – hang from the top of caves   4. Simple Subject – dog / Predicate – barked at the cat
for an hour   5. Simple Subject – class / Predicate – is best   6. Simple Subject – spiders / Predicate – spin beautiful webs
7. Simple Subject – Cindy / Predicate – drank all of the juice   8. Simple Subject – she / Predicate – was late for dinner

Pg. 141-142 Phrases #1 and #2
Answers will vary.

Pg. 143 Phrases #3
1. Prep   2. Verb   3. Prep   4. Verb   5. Prep   6. Prep   7. Verb   8. Prep   9. Verb   10. Verb

1. is jumping – verb / on the trampoline – prep   2. At the movies – prep / was giving – prep /   to the children - prep
3. After school – prep / will be playing – verb / with their friends – prep   4. is talking – verb / to his players –
prep / inside the dugout – prep   5. has been reading – verb / from her mom – prep / for an hour – prep
6. has rolled – verb / against the fence – prep   7. must be working – verb / on her test – prep
8. In a month – prep / will be taking – verb / on the body systems - prep

Pg. 144 Phrases #4
1. Prep   2. Verb   3. Verb   4. Prep   5. Verb   6. Prep   7. Verb   8. Prep   9. Verb   10. Prep

1. were diving – verb / into the water – prep   2. with spiky hair – prep / was squawking – verb / at the children – prep
3. At the mall – prep / in a clown – prep / was making – verb   4. had played – verb /
for five minutes – prep / at recess   5. does clean – verb / in my room – prep   6. in our class – prep /
will be making – verb / for Valentine's Day – prep   7. in the pink sweater – prep / is riding – verb
8. must be studying – verb / for her test – prep / at the library – prep

Pg. 145 Phrases #5
Answers will vary

Pg. 146 Fragment and Run-on Sentences #1
1. fragment   2. sentence   3. sentence   4. fragment   5. fragment
6. sentence   7. fragment   8. sentence   9. sentence   10. fragment

Pg. 147 Fragment and Run-on Sentences #2
1. Mom made a dress for my party. It was beautiful.   2. We went to the park. Then our teacher planted some flowers.
3. Toucans are beautiful birds. They live in the jungle.   4. Crystal went on the swing. She went very high.
5. Bobby made a sandcastle. Then he went into the water.   6. Our parrot is funny. He can tell a knock-knock joke.
7. I played in the mud. My Mom is going to be mad.   8. A button fell off of my shirt. It landed in my soup.

Pg. 148 Fragment and Run-on Sentences #3
1. S   2. F   3. RO   4. F   5. RO   6. S   7. RO   8. S   9. F   10. S   11. F   12. RO

Pg. 149 Fragment and Run-on Sentences #4
1. F   2. S   3. RO   4. S   5. F   6. RO   7. RO   8. F   9. S   10. F   11. RO   12. S

Pg. 150 Fragment and Run-on Sentences #5
   I had the best birthday party ever. All of my friends were there. We hit a piñata. We played games in our back yard. We ate ice cream with any topping we wanted. Then I got to open my presents. It was the greatest party ever.

Pg. 151 Titles or Topic Sentences #1
1. The Longest Day of the Year   2. Sentence   3. Hope Without Fear   4. My Favorite Toy
5. The Biggest Tree House in the World   6. Sentence   7. Singing a Song in the Chorus   8. Sentence

Pg. 152 Titles or Topic Sentences #2
1. Title   2. Sentence   3. Sentence   4. Title   5. Title   6. Sentence   7. Sentence   8. Title
9. Sentence   10. Title   11. Title   12. Sentence   13. Title   14. Sentence   15. Title

Pg. 153 Titles or Topic Sentences #3
1. Title   2. Sentence   3. Title   4. Sentence   5. Sentence   6. Title   7. Title   8. Sentence
9. Sentence   10. Title   11. Sentence   12. Title   13. Sentence   14. Title   15. Title

Pg. 154 Subject-Verb Agreement #1
1. Subject = Omar – Singular / buys   2. Subject = spiders – Plural / make   3. Subject = girls – Plural / are
4. Subject = water – Singular (mass noun) / is   5. Subject = customers – Plural / order
6. Subject = dad – Singular / watches   7. Subject = boys – Plural / play   8. Subject = team – Singular / was

Pg. 155 Subject-Verb Agreement #2
1. Subject = children – Plural / eat   2. Subject = teacher – Singular / is   3. Subject = Babies – Plural / climb
4. Subject = Chris – Singular / writes   5. Subject = Thomas – Singular / draws   6. Subject = We – Plural / are
7. Subject = people – Plural / wash   8. Subject = they – Plural / color   9. Subject = dress – Singular / was
10. Subject = players – Plural / throw

1. I – reads   2. I – ride   3. I – chase   4. C   5. I – barks   6. C

Pg. 156 Subject-Verb Agreement #3
1. Subject = jet – Singular / flys   2. Subject = Doctors – Plural / were   3. Subject = coaches – Plural / teach
4. Subject = boys – Plural / look   5. Subject = people – Plural / think   6. Subject = school – Singular / is
7. Subject = president – Singular / feels   8. Subject = she – Singular / touches

1. I – race   2. C   3. I – hit   4. I – tells   5. C   6. I – sings

Pg. 157 Subject-Verb Agreement #4
I. Answers will vary.
II. walk / chases / sees / runs / stand / yell / hate / think / run / is / blame / try / knock / take / is

Pg. 158-159 Chapter 6 Review
1. is jumping – verb / on the trampoline – prep   2. Before the game – prep / was talking – verb / to the players – prep
3. After lunch – prep / were playing – verb / in the sandbox – prep   4. is making – verb / in the kitchen – prep
5. will be walking – verb / to school – prep   6. in the corner – prep / is sleeping – verb / on its new bed – prep

1. S   2. F   3. RO   4. F   5. RO   6. S   7. S   8. RO   9. F

1. Title   2. Sentence   3. Sentence   4. Title   5. Title

1. I – drives   2. C   3. I – are   4. C   5. I – practice

Pg. 168 Homonyms
1. They're   2. to   3. son   4. no   5. their   6. won
7. two   8. there   9. sun   10. too   11. one   12. know

Pg. 169 Homonyms Group #1 Practice
1. know   2. won   3. sun   4. too   5. There   6. one
7. their   8. no   9. one   10. to   11. They're 12. son

Pg. 171 Homonyms Group #2
1. blew   2. steal   3. eight   4. clothes 5. hear   6. close
7. ate   8. blue   9. steel   10. here   11. ate   12. clothes

Pg. 172 Homonyms Group #2 Practice
1. ate   2. hear   3. close   4. Blue   5. here   6. clothes
7. blew   8. eight   9. hear   10. steal   11. blew   12. steel

Pg. 174 Homonyms Group #3
1. week   2. flew   3. aisle   4. weigh   5. isle   6. threw
7. weak   8. flu   9. way   10. I'll   11. through 12. aisle

Pg. 175 Homonyms Group #3
1. weigh   2. through 3. weak   4. I'll   5. flu   6. isle
7. threw   8. flew   9. aisle   10. way   11. week   12. weigh

Pg. 176 Homonyms Review #1
1. two   2. blue   3. know   4. steel   5. there   6. close   7. son   8. weak
9. to   10. no   11. steal 12. blew   13. They're 14. clothes 15. week   16. isle

Pg. 177 Homonyms Review #2
1. too   2. ate   3. hear   4. their   5. way   6. won   7. I'll   8. threw
9. eight   10. here   11. weigh 12. one   13. sun   14. through 15. aisle 16. flew

Pg. 178 Compound Words #1
1. everybody   2. handshake   3. cardboard   4. snowball   5. raindrop
6. mailbox   7. popcorn   8. blueberry   9. sailboat   10. eyesight

Pg. 179 Compound Words #2
1. sidewalk   2. meatball   3. driveway   4. trashcan   5. flashlight   6. keychain

1. bedroom   2. notebook   3. sidewalk   4. driveway   5. birthday
6. shortstop   7. baseball   8. bookshelf   9. meatball   10. paycheck

Pg. 180 Compound Words #3
1. headquarters   2. trashcan   3. oatmeal   4. flashlight   5. keychain

Pg. 181 A vs. An #1
1. an eagle / a nest   2. an aardvark / an anteater   3. a question / an answer   4. a car / an accident / an hour
5. an actor / a lawyer   6. a guide / an adventure   7. an airbag / a passenger / a crash   8. a crocodile / an alligator

Pg. 182 A vs. An #2

1. a Canadian / an American / an Asian   2. an aluminum   3. an actress / an angel   4. an ant / a picnic
5. a zebra / a monkey / an elephant   6. an apple / a good   7. a house / an apartment   8. a manager / an application
9. an orange / an avocado   10. an Eskimo / a fish / an igloo

Pg. 183 A vs. An #3

1. an ice cream / a popsicle   2. an umbrella / a hood   3. an army / a new   4. an artist / a picture / a sunset
5. an office / a letter   6. a pancake / a sausage / an egg   7. an armadillo / a predator   8. an umpire / a baseball
9. a student / an article / a field trip   10. a tree / an ax

Pg. 192 Friendly Letter #2

1. 314 Clarke Ave.   2. 5063 Fallin Ave.   3. 333 Market Street   4. 333 Desert Rd.
      Downey, CA 90801   Torrence, CA 90703   Philadelphia, PA 19103   Phoenix, AZ 70812
 December 15, 2000   March 10, 2008   July 4, 1976   April 1, 2010

Pg. 193 Friendly Letter #3

5895 Ball Street
Lakewood, CA 90715
January 1, 2004

Dear Alice,

      Be sure to indent your paragraphs in the body of your letter. In this way you will have a good looking letter.

              Yours truly,
              Cindi Rella

314 Main Street
Seal Beach, CA 90801
December 25, 2000

Dear Mary,

      I got a bike today. What did you get?

              Sincerely,
              Joseph

Pg. 194 Friendly Letter #4

#1

333 Market Street
Philadelphia, PA 19103
July 4, 1776

Dear George,
      Do you still have my pen?
              Sincerely,
              Thomas

#2

284 Black Forest Lane
Torrance, CA 90503
May 12, 1863

Dear Hansel,
      I ran out of bread crumbs. The nice lady in a house made of candy has some. Meet us in the forest.
              Your sister,
              Gretel

#3

2290 Foxhill Ave.
Arlington, TX 76014
October 12, 2004

Dear Alex,
      Thanks for the present. The poster will Look great in my room.
              Sincerely,
              Bobby

#4

258 Berry Street
Sacramento, CA 89581
August 2, 2005

Dear Kelly,
      My family will be leaving for Orlando, Florida tomorrow. We're going to visit Disneyworld. I'll send you a postcard.
              Yours truly,
              Pat Smith

#5

333 Castle Dr.
New York, New York 10128
September 13, 2002

Dear Dudley,
      I left my flying broom back in the closet. If you Send it to me here in America, I'll bring you some magic candy next summer.
              Sincerely,
              Harry

Pg. 195 Friendly Letter #5

#1

911 Beach Blvd.
Seattle, WA 98103
April 1, 2008

Dear Mom,
   I'm staying here at camp for two more weeks. April Fools! See you on Saturday.

Your son,
Ryan

#2

487 Jungle Rd.
Miami, FL 33125
June 14, 1856

Dear Tarzan,
   Thank you for the lovely time in the jungle. I loved your tree house. Say hello to your animal friends.

Your friend,
Jane

#3

8544 Sugar Street.
Reno, NV 89502
December 25, 2004

Dear Freddy,
   How was your Christmas? Mine was great. I got a new bike and a new video game.

Sincerely,
Billy

#4

915 Oak Ave
Redding, CA 96003
September 2, 2005

Dear Kyle,
   My family and I got to see the Space Shuttle land today. It was so exciting. We'll be in Yosemite tomorrow.

Yours truly,
Michael Jones

#5

621 Brady Lane
Hollywood, CA 90068
May 30, 1972

Dear Peter,
   Remember when you broke Mom's lamp? She always said not to play ball in the house.

Love,
Marsha

Pg. 199 Prefixes #1
1. rewrite / repaint / retake   2. unfair / unable / unselfish   3. pretest / preschool / prepay

Pg. 200 Prefixes #2
1. repaint   2. unfair   3. preschool   4. unselfish   5. rewrite   6. retake   7. preview   8. pretest   9. unable

Pg. 201 Prefixes #3
1. bimonthly / biannual / biweekly   2. misunderstand / misbehave / misspell   3. disagree / disrespect / disobey

Pg. 202 Prefixes #4
1. misunderstand   2. misspell   3. biannual   4. disobey   5. bimonthly   6. misbehave
7. disagree   8. biweekly   9. disrespect

Pg. 203 Prefixes #5
1. non   2. im   3. in   4. un   5. non   6. in   7. in   8. im   9. non   10. non   11. im   12. in

1. inexpensive   2. nonfiction   3. nonstop   4. insensitive   5. nonfat   6. immobile   7. inexpensive   8. impatient
9. inaccurate   10. imperfect

Pg. 204 Suffix #1
1. deepest   2. faithful   3. dirty   4. nervous   5. sensible   6. migration   7. destruction   8. strongest
9. addition   10. flexible   11. impressive   12. wonderful   13. tasteful   14. direction   15. biggest   16. sticky

Pg. 205 Suffix #2

A suffix changes the **part of speech** of a word.

1. messy   2. talkative   3. enjoyable   4. nervous   5. smartest   6. dirty   7. poisonous   8. destruction
9. careful   10. responsible   11. election   12. spacious   13. fastest   14. dirty   15. miraculous

Pg. 206 Suffix #3

1. The stars in the sky were wonderful.   2. We were nervous about the big test.   3. My shoes were dirty.
4. Heather is a creative artist.   5. That is the bravest soldier.   6. Andy is sensible.
7. The birds migration will be in winter.   8. The actor is famous.

Pg. 207 Suffix #4

1. driver   2. actor   3. beggar   4. cyclist   5. collector   6. geologist
7. helper   8. instructor   9. writer   10. gardener   11. artist   12. aviator

Pg. 208 Suffix #5

1. dancer   2. biologist   3. sailor   4. liar   5. farmer   6. author   7. dreamer   8. scientist
9. player   10. pianist   11. supervisor   12. guitarist   13. dancer   14. columnist   15. selector   16. doctor

Pg. 209 Chapter 9 Review

A prefix changes the **meaning** of a word.

1. repaint   2. unfair   3. preschool   4. bimonthly   5. misbehave
6. disobey   7. nonfat   8. imperfect   9. inexpensive   10. unhappy

A suffix changes the **part of speech** of a word.

1. breakable   2. creative / creatable /   3. dirty   4. wonderful   5. famous   6. driver
7. deepest   8. prediction / predictable   9. joyful / joyous   10. stoppable

Made in the USA
Las Vegas, NV
21 July 2023